# How To Pray for Your Children

## ABOUT THE AUTHOR

Rev. Erwin E. Prange is associate pastor of a large Lutheran church as well as associate pastoral counselor at the Center for Christian Psychotherapy in Roseville, Minnesota. Having pastored and counseled in Brooklyn, N.Y., Montana, and Johns Hopkins Hospital in Baltimore, Maryland, he is eminently qualified to share on the subject of intercession for troubled families.

# How To Pray for Your Children

## Erwin E. Prange

Bethany Fellowship INC.
MINNEAPOLIS, MINNESOTA 55438

Scripture quotations are taken from the Revised Standard Version
of the Bible.

Published by Bethany Fellowship, Inc.
6820 Auto Club Road, Minneapolis, Minnesota 55438

Printed in the United States of America

---

**Library of Congress Cataloging in Publication Data**

Prange, Erwin E.
   How to pray for your children.

   Bibliography: p.
   1. Prayer. 2. Family—Religious life. I. Title.
BV210.2.P63   248'.3   79-17382
ISBN 0-87123-162-X

---

# TABLE OF CONTENTS

# INTRODUCTION

There's a time to get married and a time not to get married. And right now is not the time! The odds are all stacked against happiness. Today's bride has only a 50% chance of staying married and a 50% chance of having a faithful husband. Even if she does stay married and is fortunate enough to have a faithful husband, the chances for romantic love and solid marital contentment are very low. According to a national news survey reported on December 6, 1978, family problems due to alcohol alone have doubled in the past four years. One-fourth of all families are adversely affected by problem drinking, and one-third of all divorces are blamed on alcohol abuse.

Families are also disintegrating. Ninety percent of all teenagers have tried some kind of illegitimate drug. Thirty-one percent of all households are headed by single parents only, and in 60% of all homes the children are forced to raise themselves while both parents work.

Depression, insecurity, drugs and the occult govern our times. One-third of all births to teenagers in the U.S. are illegitimate and in Washington, D.C., the figure is 51%. The number of young people involved in alcoholism, suicide, crime and schizophrenia is rising rapidly, while the average age of those involved is dropping frighteningly fast. Already suicide ranks second as a cause of death among college students.

According to the prevailing philosophy, this is a time for singles. Lifetime commitment is becoming less and less attractive in the midst of global insecurity and explosive change. The number of men and women between the ages of 20 to 24 who voluntarily choose the single life-style has exploded in the seventies.

The family represents a long-term commitment caught in a tidal wave of social, economic and technological change. Women's Lib, television and secular humanism all threaten the 19th century family role models that many have been living out. The moral capital of basic Christianity on which this nation was founded is all but exhausted. Moral relativism, in which there is no absolute evil or good is slowly but surely taking over. The church, too, is in a state of transition and turmoil. It represents eternal commitment in a time when a generation scarcely lasts three years. We are all in an identity crisis. Like the people in Greenwich Village in Manhatten, we have to reinvent ourselves every day to keep up with a changing society.

We are not helpless, however. There is something vital and powerful that can and must be done. It is called the Family Covenant Prayer. This book shares that discovery and how it affected my own family as well as the families of hundreds of others. Salvation in the Bible is not merely concerned with the soul after death. The Greek word *soteria* embraces the whole man—body, soul and spirit—for time and eternity. Salvation includes healing, wholeness, deliverance, protection and prosperity as well as eternal spiritual welfare. Beyond that, salvation is more than an individual prize; God's covenant is with the family. The American ideal of rugged individualism is partly illusion. "God setteth the solitary in families." He deals with the family, not just the individual. This book is born out of the cry of a father's broken heart, "How can I be truly saved if a part of me is cut off from God forever?" Or, as Tennyson puts into the mouth of a mother, "What does my immortal soul mean to me if my boy goes to the flames?" To these haunting cries, the Scripture answers over and over again, "Believe in the Lord Jesus, and you will be saved, you and your household" (Acts 16:31-33). It's not an answer to rest upon but a challenge to be prayed day and night. Give Him and give yourself no rest day and night, but pour out your heart like water before the Lord because He has sworn it by His mighty arm (see Isa. 62:6-8). "Arise, cry out in the night . . . pour out your heart like water before the presence of the Lord! Lift your hands to him for the lives of your children" (Lam. 2:19).

"For this reason I bow my knees before the Father, from whom every family in heaven and on earth is named" (Eph. 3:14, 15). "Jesus, you came into the world through the human family; your birth and death were cradled by a mother's love. We name before you now our earthly families and ask you to include them in the heavenly one."

# Chapter 1

# BALTIMORE

*Heavenly Father, we believe that there are indeed sermons in stones and prayers in babbling brooks. Enlighten the eyes of our hearts to hear and to see what you are saying around and within us. Let the inarticulate cries of our spirits form words that reach your ears. Teach us constantly to ask, to seek, and to knock and not to grow bitter or to wallow in self-pity. Forgive us, Father, for not praying or caring enough, for failing to claim all the riches of your promises. Send your Spirit to teach us how to pray the Family Covenant. May He pray it within when our lips and minds grow forgetful and silent. May nothing you want to give us or do for us go unclaimed for lack of word or thought.*

*In Jesus' Name. Amen.*

It was during my second week in Baltimore that it really hit me. Why did I have this terrible feeling of oppression that I had never known during all the years in Brooklyn? It was a Sunday afternoon and I was making a sick call in an all-black section of South Baltimore. This was nothing new for me. I had ministered to blacks and Puerto Ricans for fourteen years in New York. I was not aware of either fear or prejudice, but suddenly something was bugging me terribly. All at once it hit me: mine was the only white face for miles around! I was a tiny but conspicuous white dot in a sullen black sea. There was both hostility and wonder in the air. Where did this stupid white priest come from? Didn't he know that this neighborhood was for blacks only? The

Montana license on my car suggested that I must be hope-
lessly lost. "A funny thing happened to me on the way to
Great Falls last week, I got lost and ended up in downtown
Baltimore."

In New York there were ghettoes and ethnic neighbor-
hoods but there was always some kind of mix. No matter
where you went or what color you were, you could always
find a similar face. New York was the mirror of the world,
but Baltimore was the Mason Dixon Line, the Civil War
and the slave ships forever frozen in miles and miles of red
brick row-houses with polished sandstone steps.

Why didn't I see this on my first trip down? How could I
come from a church with twelve millionaires and a radio
station to a hundred-year-old telephone building and a
scattered, all-black congregation? Suddenly everything
about Baltimore and St. Matthew's congregation depressed
me. The community center reminded me of all the urban
programs that had failed. White surburban guilt was forever making futile symbolic gestures in the ghetto. Behind
all the high-powered spiritual words I read the real truth. I
had taken a job that nobody else wanted and now I was
stuck with it in the name of the Lord. In New York and
Montana I had felt a unity among the clergy. Here it
seemed to be every man for himself. I felt lonely and be-
trayed. The war between the races wasn't over. It would
never be over as long as the flesh existed. Christianity
didn't really make a difference after all. I had been be-
trayed by my own idealism. This was the end of the inner
city road. That empty, vandalized community center stood
for all the broken dreams about integration and the broth-
erhood of man.

What about the Spirit? Would He move against the
whole cultural stream? It seemed that everybody, black
and white, charismatic and non-charismatic, was looking

on waiting for me to pass a miracle. My depression deep-ened—I wanted to just go to bed and pull the covers over my head. God had taken me all the way through Brooklyn and then round about by way of Montana, only to drop me off on a deadend street.

There was a way out. It was one that I had used before in New York—hospital chaplaincy. As soon as a program opened up at Lutheran Hospital in Baltimore, I signed up as a chaplain intern. It was a good program and I enjoyed being back on the wards again. The only trouble was I made too many calls. The first time the hospital chaplain asked me how many bedside calls I had made that week I said, "Two hundred."

He almost fainted. "Why that's more than I made in a year," He replied. "How many did you pray for?" He asked somewhat cautiously.

I replied, "All of them."

From that moment on he knew he had a charismatic problem on his hands, and I knew that I had found my place again in the kingdom even if it was in Baltimore.

## Chapter 2

# GIANT MARBLE JESUS

*Heavenly Father, forgive us for failing to see your hand in all things. We know that your strength is made perfect in weakness but, oh, how we hate weakness! Forgive us for failing to love those nearest to us and for failing to see their hurts as we reach out to all the world. Let love begin at home. May the Word be made flesh first in our own families. Jesus, you came into the world through a human family. You suffered all the frustration with those who know us too well. You suffered the hurt of failure with those nearest and dearest. Your own brothers did not believe in you. Holy Spirit, let the love of Jesus be poured into our hearts from above. We cannot love as we should on our own. Baptize us with divine agape love.*

*In Jesus' Name. Amen.*

It began in Montana. She was the eldest, tall, dark and slender like her mother. The boys began to gather when she was barely 16. I overreacted, and she began to act out her rebellion. The boys seemed to represent everything that her father was against. It was an effective and public way of getting even with Daddy for neglecting her all those hectic years in Brooklyn. The last one was the worst. I threw him out of the house several times and then he was picked up on drug charges. We had a confrontation. "You will never marry her," I said.

"When she is 18 we have plans and you can't stop us," he said.

"That's right, but the Lord will." I didn't know at that heated moment how prophetic those words would prove to be.

He followed us to Baltimore. I tried to get help from the police but they were useless. There were confrontations and hard words. I was absolutely right, so why talk about love or or understanding or forgiveness at all? I could have shot him—and almost did at least once.

Suddenly she was 18. She packed and sped off to California to be married. Tears, pleas and prayer were all in vain. We wept on each other's shoulders and said good-bye, perhaps forever. Margie and I were not going to be at the wedding and would probably have no part in her future at all. Margie and the boys drove her to Kansas and Texas to say good-bye to the grandparents. Diane and I stayed behind in Baltimore. It all happened so suddenly that I didn't have time to think or even to feel. How could my baby do this to me? God, you must have been looking the other way.

My work seemed mechanical. It was difficult to concentrate. After a routine day at Lutheran Hospital, I went to Johns Hopkins Hospital to call on some of my members. As I was walking from the parking lot to the hospital something broke. I began to mourn—far, far worse than for the dead. It was an eternal mourning for the lost.

Inside the hospital—I scarcely knew how I got there—I paused before the giant marble statue of Jesus in the entrance. In a mist of tears I stood to one side and began a silent dialogue with the soft brown marble. "Giant marble Jesus, do you know how I feel? How can I give spiritual help and comfort to others when my own heart is breaking? The pain is too great! I don't know where to go with it. Tell me, giant Jesus, how can I be truly saved if a part of me is cut off from God forever? A billion, billion years from now she will still be a part of me, and I will be embarrassing heaven with my tears. What does my eternal soul matter if she goes to the fire? You can't let her marry that unbeliever. Jesus, you can't! I won't let you!" The tears were flowing freely by now but I didn't care. As I walked down the long corridors of Johns Hopkins, everyone stared at me. They must have thought, "Things are pretty tough in this hospital if even the chaplains are crying."

Johns Hopkins Hospital is one of the greatest in the world. Every department of medicine is covered. The new additions have almost swallowed up the original buildings with their huge oil portraits of famous physicians. Johns Hopkins represents the highest in medical and scientific achievement and is surrounded by the total social and economic failure of the ghetto. People come there from all over the world, yet the deepest and most hopeless human misery lies at its doorstep. Wasn't that a parable about my own situation? "He saved others but himself he cannot save." "Physician, heal thyself."

At home in my office I fell on my knees and sobbed. I was glad that no one was home except Diane and that I had no place to go that evening. Males of German ancestry are taught never to show their emotions and so they grow up fixated at the emotional age of three. There was a lot of catching up that night, as God and I had it out in that tiny office on the Alameda. In that close encounter of the ultimate kind, all the masks came off.

"God, you can't let her marry an unbeliever. I won't let you. Neither of us will ever see her again." I was on my face on the floor. My tears were staining the rug. God spoke; it was not the earthquake or the fire, but a still small voice within: "Believe on the Lord Jesus Christ and you will be saved and your household." "Yes, God, I believe," I said. "You have sworn it and you cannot lie. You have sworn the most sacred oath by your own lips, 'As I live, says the Lord.'

Father, you can't let this happen. I won't let you break your promise to me! Your word is true, your covenants are unbreakable. Now make me believe it. Prove it to me!"

I don't know how long I lay there, but I was stiff and hungry when I got off the floor. Diane was calling for me to come and eat. She was the "elder brother," the younger sister who had never gone away. In my tears for the prodigal, I had almost forgotten about her. She had never broken my heart and I had never really poured out my soul in prayer for her. When she was born in the midst of a hurricane in St. Louis, I named her Diane after the storm. Jokingly I had said, "If the second one is also a girl, I won't even bring her home." I first saw her when she was 15 minutes old. She was angry and then she cried for a solid year. She knew that first moment when I looked at her that she was supposed to be a boy.

On the following day I finished early at the hospital, made a few calls on parishioners, and came home in time for dinner. The house was quiet. When I entered the kitchen I was greeted by a very large black bird. I was just making a mental note to ask myself, "What is this big black bird doing in the kitchen?" when I heard a faint cry. It seemed to be coming from my office.

Diane was crying, "Help, help me please, somebody. Daddy, is that you? Be careful or it will get you, too!"

I had visions of her being raped, stabbed and bleeding to death. Maybe the ones who did it were still around. I couldn't find a gun so I grabbed a baseball bat.

"Diane, Diane, here I come! Is there anybody else around?" A thousand horrible pictures flashed through my mind. The faint cries grew louder, "Help, help, help!" I opened the office door expecting the worst. It was—the worst female hysteria I had ever seen. Diane was crying, screaming, trying to phone all at the same time. She kept knocking the phone to the floor where it finally rested with a few protesting beeps.

"Daddy, Daddy, close the door or it will get you, too! I was sitting in front of the fireplace when it came down the chimney and grabbed me by the hair. I fought it for thirty minutes and finally managed to escape and lock myself in here."

"Whoa, hold it. What and where and who is this 'it'?" I grabbed the bat and prepared to do battle.

"The bird, the big black bird. It clawed my face and tried to claw my eyes out. It's some kind of demon or devil, I know!"

"We'll see about that." I walked out the door and there it was in the dining room. I swung from the floor. It was a home run! The bird dropped dead at my feet. It looked like a crow or a raven. Anyhow, it was very, very dead and I threw the remains in the garbage can and tried to calm Diane.

Diane had always lived under the domination of her older sister. Karen was born first sergeant, and every childhood photo shows her putting Diane through the manual of arms. The big black bird was symbolical. Its death symbolized that the ancestral bondage, against which every family struggles, was beginning to be released in the Prange family.

Just then the phone rang. It was Margie calling from Kansas. "We're coming home, all of us." The Lord had reached down and pulled the prodigal off the plane in Dallas and now He was bringing her home. The husband-to-be called the next day from Los Angeles and asked what had happened. "Remember what I told you in Montana?" I said. "Well, the Lord has acted. You will never see her again." And he never did. That door of her life was forever closed, and the Lord opened up a new door for me.

That moment each of us in a way was released from some kind of interpersonal bondage. Karen was set free from rebellion and Diane was set free from Karen's domination. From that day on the girls and I had a different relationship with each other. It was far from perfect, but there had been a breakthrough. This is the kind of release which must take place again and again in every family. The key to it all is the Family Covenant.

## Chapter 3

# WHAT CAN WE DO ABOUT MOTHER?

*Forgive us, Father, for being so selfish about our salvation. Open our eyes to the healing powers of your covenant love. Make our families true households of faith where your transforming grace is shared with every member of the family. We thank you for mothers who are bearers of the eternal Word. We thank you for the mother in whose lap we first heard the gospel and at whose knee we breathed our first prayers. We remember your mother and every mother who taught us the concrete meaning of divine love. Lord, make our families living parables of spiritual truth. Let them be earthly symbols of heavenly fellowship.*

*In Jesus' Name. Amen.*

Tip and his brother Bob were a paradox that blew all social theory. They were white boys who grew up in the heart of one of Baltimore's black ghettoes. They managed to contradict every role model and confound all psychological learning theory. In the midst of crime and delinquency, they became eagle scouts. Surrounded by indifference and hostility to religion, they were very spiritual teenagers. They were neither sissy nor withdrawn but were athletes and leaders. Tip and Bob seemed to be what every parent dreams and prays that his teenagers will become. What was the secret? Reverse psychology, predestination or just plain luck? I have known many prominent religious leaders whose children were an outright embarrassment to them because their lives contradicted everything their father taught and stood for. Now the contradiction was in reverse. The family covenant also works in reverse as I was about to discover.

I had sort of inherited Tip and Bob when I took over the pastorate of Our Saviour Lutheran Church in Baltimore. This was after St. Matthew's and Our Saviour merged in 1973. They were the youth leaders—in fact, they were just about the only youth left in the church. They also led the various scout programs still functioning in the parish.

We had started a regular Friday night healing service. The boys came into my office late on Friday after the service was finished. Without introduction or preliminary they blurted out, "Pastor, what can we do about our mother?"

"Why, what's she doing?" I asked almost automatically.

"She drinks," they both blushed.

"How much?" I asked, wondering if they were pietists.

"Sometimes a quart a day. She hides it. Sometimes she blacks out and falls down. We can't talk to her about it."

"Would it help if I talked to her?" I felt the need to do something. This is a problem that affects most pastors when they counsel.

"No, she don't like you." It's always a little deflating to a pastoral ego when he discovers that one of his parishioners doesn't exactly adore him. The fan club is vocal and visible, but the knockers tend to go underground a bit.

After I had straightened out my self-image a bit, I suggested calmly, "Why don't we pray the family covenant for her?"

"What's that, Pastor?"

After I had explained, we went back into the church and the boys knelt at the altar rail. I laid hands on both their heads and began to pray.

"Heavenly Father, remember your family covenant and

hear the prayer of these two sons. Heal their mother of acute alcoholism and bring her close to you. Send your Spirit into the heart of their father that he may have a hunger and a thirst for the Word like that of his sons. I thank you for these boys, for their faith and for their love. I know that you have called them and their whole household. Complete their calling and salvation by bringing the whole family into a living relationship with you. Let them give themselves and you no rest day and night but pour out their heart like water before you. Because you have made a sworn covenant with these two boys and you cannot lie." Amen.

We prayed in this way every Friday night after the healing service. Meanwhile, I told them not to breathe a word to their mother or anyone else about what we were praying for. For many times I had been told, "Who asked you to pray for me? What made you think I needed prayer?" Prayer implies need, and showing need is a threat to pride and status.

Tip, Bob and I prayed this way for about five or six months. Suddenly their mother stopped drinking entirely. Scarcely a word was said and to this day she doesn't know about those family covenant prayers that sobered her up. Shortly afterwards their father quietly accepted the Lord and started coming to church. Tip will soon be in his last year at a Lutheran seminary. The Lord is able and willing to do abundantly above what we ask or think, or imagine. Once we start claiming His covenant promises we won't be able to turn off all the blessings.

Tip has already been called a Lutheran Billy Graham. He is surely destined for spiritual greatness because the hand of the Lord is mighty upon him. If the years in Baltimore produced nothing more than Tip, they would still be worth all the pain and frustration.

## Chapter 4

## MARK

*Heavenly Father, you spared not your own Son but gave Him up freely for us all. How much more will you not with Him freely give us all things? Father, we believe that Jesus was your Isaac, the highest and best of your love. We thank you for that heavenly Son and also for the earthly sons you have given us in trust. We are spiritually deaf, dumb and blind. You need to sign your love into our hands. In the midst of life's deepest tragedies, you speak of a love that is stronger than death, or a love that will not let us go. We thank you that through the human family you have imprinted in our hearts the full meaning of self-giving love. May the broken heart of God speak plainly through the brokenness of our loved ones. Jesus, we believe that every knife cuts you and every pain is your pain and every cry yours, too. As we feel the pain of our family member, so you feel ours, too. Don't waste, Lord, don't waste a single cry or tear or prayer but put them all on your back on the cross and make them redemptive.*

*In Jesus' Name. Amen.*

For a while it seemed as if he wasn't meant to be born. Several times Margie's body threatened to abort him and twice during the pregnancy she had to be hospitalized. But she managed to carry the child to full term. This time more than ever we were haunted with the fear, "What if the baby is deformed or retarded? Maybe he will grow up to be a criminal. Perhaps God was trying to tell us something and he wasn't supposed to be born at all."

But the time finally came, as all times do. Dr. Mascola called from Lutheran Hospital in Brooklyn at 3:00 a.m. "It's a boy!"

Half asleep and half unbelieving I answered, "Doctor, you must have the wrong number; you know I have had nothing but girls so far."

"Yes, but that was another doctor in St. Louis. I deliver boys on order, just come and see!"

He was right. That morning when I walked into Lutheran Hospital nursery ward, I was greeted by a boy baby with a shock of stiff black hair. His skin looked dark, too. At first I thought that Margie and some Puerto Rican woman had somehow mixed up their babies. I started looking for a Puerto Rican baby with blond hair and blue eyes. But everything was in order. He was mine. Just dark like his mother.

Immediately I sent a flock of telegrams. The first-born son is an even greater event for the father than the first-born. The telegram to my sister in Pembroke, Ontario, was supposed to read, "Dark-skinned black-haired 8 lb. boy born to Margie in Lutheran Hospital." Someone in the telegraph office omitted "haired." My sister Mary is still trying to live it down. She has preserved the telegram as evidence.

Mark was first brought in to Margie while I was in the hospital. When she gave him his bottle, he actually smiled. It was a smile of greeting and recognition as if to say, "Well, it was a long, hard trip, but I'm glad to be here. I'm also glad that you are my parents." He's been smiling ever since. He has always had that positive approach, even though we let him go to school and grow up in one of the nation's toughest ghettoes.

There could hardly be a greater contrast between my boyhood and Mark's. I was born in a little river town in Arkansas at the end of the road. I didn't see a train until I was twelve. My boyhood was 19th-century Tom Sawyer. Mark grew up under the sound of the Broadway and Myrtle Ave. L's in Brooklyn. Instead of hunting and fishing, he played stickball among the garbage cans. Instead of swimming in the White River, he dodged trucks on Bushwick Avenue.

We both grew up dangerously—in radically different kinds of ways. One thing we did have in common in our boyhoods: exposure to violence. Mark grew up surrounded by gang warfare and routinely saw bloodshed by switch-blades and zip guns. I had witnessed shotgun duels to the death between feuding rivermen. The boys in my school in Arkansas fought not with fists but with shotguns.

Life in Brooklyn was so hectic and demanding that I scarcely knew Mark or his younger brother, Stephen, until we moved to Libby, Montana. In the wild, beautiful wilderness around Libby, I taught the boys how to shoot, how to hunt and how to fish. I went back to my childhood in Arkansas and there we met as boys together. A bond was formed that hasn't been completed all the way, but was never broken. The boys took to the new life-style immediately. The Brooklyn identity was shed almost overnight, although the accent wasn't. They became instant outdoorsmen and hunters. It had been in their blood all along.

Baltimore was something of a setback. Several times the boys were attacked by gangs, and they held me responsible for bringing them back into the urban jungle. I tried to make it up to them by going on camping trips to the Skyline Drive in Virginia and to Cape Hatteras in the summer. Those were the times of the closest togetherness we had ever known in our lives. The more we were rained out and half frozen, the more we felt like a family. We could not communicate in the language of theology, but the forest and the sea caught us up into the common language of mankind. The scars of the asphalt jungle began to heal.

Suddenly the magic years were gone. The boys were almost grown and did things with their friends. Dad was still necessary but more and more irrelevant.

Parents have so little time to relate to their children. Sometimes we act as if the relationship would last forever. The trivia of everyday living crowd out and pre-empt the fleeting moments of parent-child togetherness. We are ships that pass in the night and yet we are bound together by an eternal covenant.

There was another hour and another place where we would meet. It was not Cape Hatteras or Skyline Drive, but the valley of the shadow of death. At the brink of the grave I was to learn the deeper meaning of being a father. Once more the Lord would teach me painfully in my own family the meaning of the family covenant.

Margie and I had just arrived at the Curtis Hotel in Minneapolis. It had been a hard two-day drive from Baltimore, but now we were prepared to relax before the International Lutheran Conference on the Holy Spirit began. But our little world was suddenly shattered by a phone message. Mark had been seriously injured in an auto accident the night before. He was lying near death in the shock trauma ward of Maryland General Hospital in Baltimore.

The last time I spoke at the Prayer and Praise gathering at Trinity Lutheran Church in Joppatown, Maryland, something caused me to see this accident. I said to the group, "Twice now Stephen has almost been killed in a freak accident. I wonder why nothing has happened to Mark so far?" We prayed that the Lord would protect Stephen since he seemed to be under some kind of demonic attack. Nothing more happened to him but I failed to pray against Mark's accident. The Lord didn't want it to happen. He was trying to warn me but I missed the message.

Evil is not inevitable; we are sometimes given a partial revelation about some future tragic event in order that we may specifically pray against it!

Somehow we managed to get through to Mark on the phone. He was still conscious. Because of the severe internal injuries they could not administer anesthesia. Mark and I had never really been close spiritually. Like many family members there were so many conflicting and overlapping relationships that the spiritual was compromised. We were embarrassed to share what had often been a purely authoritarian structure. But now we had to confront one another over a long distance line. Again the masks came off. It is through our children that the Lord reaches us. For the first time I knew how I really felt about Mark. At the brink of death I knew for the first time what it meant to be a father.

## Chapter 5

# PRAY, DAD, PRAY!

*Jesus, we thank you that you can share with us all human pain and need. You are the great high priest who understands and loves and is able to help in every need. Help us to go out from ourselves so that the hurts of others may be at least as important as our own. Show us how to stand in the other person's place and thus be true intercessors like you. We thank you for our families and for that natural human love which points beyond itself to your perfect love. We thank you for your constant intercession which covers and completes our feeble prayers. Let us and our families be caught up into that eternal intercession from the cross. May the life of God in your blood shed on Calvary cry out continuously for our needs and our sins. We thank you for your perfect intercession which cries; "Father, don't punish them, punish me. Father, don't see them, look at me; let me take their place." Jesus, make us family intercessors willing to stand in the loved one's place.*

*In Your Name. Amen.*

Mark had always been daring and reckless. He grew up dodging gangs, muggers and trucks in Brooklyn, New York, and somehow his normal anxiety quotient did not develop. He did not seem to be overly interested in intellectual and spiritual things. When he was in the first grade in the Brooklyn ghetto, he would be beaten up for even pretending to be interested in his school work. The same thing happened to me when I was in the first grade in Arkansas, but I had a giant retarded bodyguard who was 6' 2" and in the third grade. Underneath his protecting wing, I read everything I could lay my hands on and no one dared touch me. There was only one problem—my bodyguard's hobby was skinning skunks!

Once while I was acting principal of St. Mark's school in Brooklyn, I glanced at Mark's records. His I.Q. score shocked and depressed me. According to tests he had taken while in the first grade, his I.Q. was 94—dull normal. How could this be, when his mother's and my score were much higher? Perhaps God meant for him to be aborted so that we would be spared the pain and embarrassment of a retarded child.

I kept this information to myself for a long time. I did talk to his teacher and she gave me the bad news that he had been the slowest one in his kindergarten class. I tried to share some of this with Margie, but she would become furious every time I brought it up. After all, she was a kindergarten teacher and she ought to know who was smart and who was dumb. Never, never try to tell a parent that his or her child is less than brilliant!

Mark's high school record was not particularily reassuring. In Montana and in Baltimore I found myself in frequent dialog with his teachers and principals. In Montana, where I preached over the radio every Sunday morning, the school officials seemed to rejoice in reporting to me the latest truancy of my son. "Like you said the other Sunday, Reverend, we've got to set a good example for our children. Our children hear what we do and not what we say— preaching begins in the home."

"All right, go on rub it in," I would think to myself. After all, who can raise children in a goldfish bowl? High visibility fathers are a challenge and a temptation to creative children who want to get even before an audience.

When Mark enrolled in Towson State College in Towson, Maryland, I was very pessimistic. It looked like a waste of money to me, but the family had agreed that each child was entitled to at least two years of full tuition in the college of his or her choice. One day in a moment of total frustration I called Mark "stupid." This was a word that I was never going to be allowed to forget. Its implications will echo throughout eternity. Family history tends to repeat itself in dramatic detail. When I was six my father spanked me for reading too much. "I don't want my son to be a bookworm; I want him to be practical. Go out and play like other children, learn to use your hands. People with education and book knowledge are stupid. The really smart people are those with brains in their hands and feet as well as in their heads." This was his favorite speech and his deepest misbelief. He himself was a natural mathematical genius who had quit school in the seventh grade to become a farmer and a businessman. All of his thirteen children were gifted, but my two sisters and I were the only ones to get college degrees. The three of us went to college late in life because the misbelief that brainwashed Dad's children and grandchildren also created unconscious resistance to formal education in us.

That spanking I got for reading was no doubt in part responsible for my reading some 25,000 books during the next 55 years. Dad did not mean for it to be reverse psychology, but that is the way it worked out. "You meant it for whatever but God turned it into good." Thus God can redeem not only our acts but also our motives.

The very same thing happened with Mark. From the moment that I said that magic word "stupid," he was transformed from a goof-off into a scholar. Never in the history of human psychology did unintentional reverse psychology work so well. From that moment on Mark became a straight 4.0 student. He has maintained a perfect scholastic record at Bethel College while preparing for a graduate program in clinical psychology. It's a constant miracle because, when we look at his writing and spelling, he seems almost illiterate. The ghosts and gaps of ghetto schooling still haunt his creative mind, but the gifts shine through nevertheless.

A large part of conscience is anxiety. Fear of consequences, getting caught and being punished doth make saints of us all. Mark's low anxiety level plus his ghetto upbringing had produced a very flexible conscience. He tended to be something of a sociopath and a con artist. For this reason he and I had a hard time sharing spiritually. My public image plus flashbacks of guilt about my past made it rather difficult for me to accept him. Sometimes in my fantasy I would pretend that there really had been a baby switch at Lutheran Hospital in Brooklyn. I wondered how that unknown Puerto Rican mother was enjoying her blond, blue-eyed, genius saint, while I raised her stupid, dark-skinned sociopath.

But now was the time for truth. Mark was dying and he and I had to communicate on all levels. Whenever he shared his pain and his wish to die, something would die inside of me, too. Who could I blame? The boy who drove too fast, or the stupid juvenile game of chicken that caused them to pass at high speed on a blind curve? Could I blame Mark for going on a ride with a stranger who had a reputation for reckless driving? Could I blame God or the devil or myself for not praying against the disaster that I so plainly saw coming? In my helpless grief I wanted to strike out at somebody or something. I felt guilty for all my rejection of Mark—real or projected. Mostly I felt guilty for the things I hadn't done or said. I felt guilty for the father I hadn't been to the boy whom I scarcely knew who was about to be taken from me.

But now we could meet on the battlefield of prayer. I began to understand what Abraham went through when God asked him to sacrifice Isaac. He might have thought, "God, take me, not him. I've lived my life. Or take Ishamel, he's only half legitimate and he's not the son of the promise. How about Sarah? All she does is get me into trouble with her pretty face and her big mouth. But you can't want Isaac. If he dies, nothing that you've done for me really has any meaning. God, you can't be serious. You can have anything or anyone except Isaac."

I could also begin to understand Calvary a little better. Christ was the Isaac of God—the highest and best of God, the essence of His love incarnate. This time no angel came to stay the hand of death. God's Isaac died a real death on the altar of the cross just across from Mount Moriah where the first Isaac was spared. "Will he not then with him freely give us all things?" Did this include giving us back our Isaacs? Isaac—Mark, I can't stay the hand of death, but I can offer myself as another target. God, let me lay myself on the altar in his place!"

At this time a deeper understanding of intercession began to form. The intercessor must be able to love enough to take the other's place. The intercessor must be able to say and to mean it, "Let me take his place; take me instead." Only a father or a mother or God is able to say that. Again and again, I offered myself in Mark's place. The Lord knew it wasn't just a dramatic gesture. He knew I really meant it. Then I also knew why the family covenant was so important. As Mark was a part of me, so are we a part of the Heavenly Father through Jesus our brother. We will do anything for that person who is a part of ourselves, including dying for them. This is the bond of the intercessor, a prayer covenant which must be answered. This is an offer that God can't refuse.

## Chapter 6

# A TIME FOR INTERCESSION

Every once in a while I run across one of my old class-mates from Aviation Cadet Class 43-E at Maxwell Field, Alabama. Many of those who are still alive are retired Air Force Colonels. Most of them are dead. They died at the controls of bombers over Pleosti, Rumania, or Schweinfurt, Germany. As I look back now, it all seemed like such a waste. Three-fourths of the planes and crews were lost over Pleosti. Why? So that the oil fields could reopen, two months later, bigger and better than ever? They were mag-nificent young men, the cream of America, sacrificed on the altar of one foul-up after another. All that youth, all that patriotism, and all that training—just to die for a high-level miscalculation. Studies we did in Germany after the war indicated that the bombings might have actually prolonged the war. They were America's kamikaze flyers—brave, skilled and futile.

One pilot who was scheduled to be offered up early in the war was absent. He was so plagued with airsickness that he finally and reluctantly grounded himself. I didn't know the still small voice. The earthquakes and the fire were everywhere, but one thing was certain: the canals in my ears responsible for maintaining balance were constant-ly overreacting to violent aerobatics. One way or another the Lord gets His point across, if not by mystic revelation, then by smelly regurgitation. I didn't even know Him then, but already He had other plans for my life. A blueprint drawn before the foundation of the world was beginning to unfold. I had been predestined in love before all worlds and now the details of thought, word and deed, downsitting and uprising were being filled in. But first the stage had to be set.

The Lord's hand was certainly on my destiny, but I found it increasingly hard to believe that He had dealt himself a hand in the chaotic destruction that had been so gently named armed conflict. For almost five years in England, France, Germany and Western Europe, World War II and its aftermath unfolded itself before my wondering eyes. Man's supreme madness, the stuff of which history and nightmares are made, presents far, far too much input to be processed by our human psyche. I'm sure the angels are puzzled too. Only God can make sense out of it all. Or can He? Does He perhaps hide himself behind a cloud of glory and ignore what His greatest failures are up to? Frequently I was lovingly shrouded in the gentle mist of captured alcohol and didn't care. Who can possibly understand, when all human values are suddenly reversed and all things, including chaplain's prayers, are dedicated to total destruction?

I can remember lying behind a big tree dodging bullets from a German fighter plane and watching a thousand-plane daylight raid over Stuttgart, Germany. It was the last great U.S. raid on the city before it was captured. It had all the quality of a dream or of a movie. Bombs fell and buildings floated in the air. Anti-aircraft fire and fighter planes struck down bombers which drifted lazily to the ground or exploded in midair. Sometimes there would be parachutes as the crews of the bombers leaped into their own holocaust. It was all so far away and so high in the sky. The bombers were toys and the city was a movie set. It couldn't be real, could it? But it was and for two years I lived in the rubble that had been Stuttgart. In June of the following year I walked past a bomb shelter that had received a direct hit from a thousand-pound bomb. They hadn't even bothered to remove the twenty-five-hundred bodies. The sick, sweet smell of death poisoned the rainy June day. In the midst of life we are in death.

God looked down and saw all of it. But from where? Was He far, far behind the battle lines like some general or down in the foxholes and shelters where the action was? Did, as Helmut Thielicke suggests, every bullet strike Him and every bomb blast Him, too? Did He in the solidarity of the cross hear every feeble cry and feel every throb of pain? Did He indeed see every tear and share every death as His own loss? Then how could He possibly bear it? Leslie Weatherhead describes a dream in which the archangels and the cherubim look down upon the earthly scene. Nothing escapes their celestial gaze. At one and the same time the joy of heaven is on their faces and the pain of earth is in their eyes. That mingled look of joy and pain was more than mortal man could bear and so he awoke—it was only a dream, a dream too much for flesh and blood.

How did God govern all of this? Years later I read in Luther that God governs the church from the inside with the gospel and the chaos from the outside with His wrath. As in the precreation eternity, the Spirit broods creatively above the chaos, seeking to redeem and heal. God was certainly the Lord of His church and of His own, but wasn't Satan the God of this world? In what sense was God Lord of history, of chaos and of war? It was many years later before I was to find out.

There were greater and deeper puzzles about the war—like the Dunkirk evacuation for example. This took place before I got to England, but I heard many vivid personal descriptions of it. The German panzers had burst through the low countries with lightning speed. The British Expeditionary Force of almost half a million men was helplessly trapped between the German tanks and the English Channel. It looked hopeless, but a sudden and unexpected storm held up the Germans for five or six hours. In the meantime the cry went through all of England: "To the boats, to the boats, everything that floats toward Dunkirk!" Suddenly the English Channel, that wild and stormy body of water, became a sea of glass. Even rowboats could cross and did. The B.E.F. was rescued. It was another crossing of the Red Sea, but where was Moses?

The next great miracle was the battle of Britain. Except for the V-1s and the V-2s, this was also over when I got there. I saw the ruins of London, Coventry and Manchester and heard personal tales of horror from the survivors. As we were to learn later, Britain had been practically beaten to her knees by the German Air Force. The last British fighter plane was on the ground. The anti-aircraft of the time was practically useless against night bombers. England lay helpless and exposed to a great German bomber fleet on the way. Suddenly just fifty miles away from London, the Germans turned towards the Mediterranean. England was spared again. The angel of death had passed over, but why? Who had painted blood upon the doorposts? Surely something had made the victorious German bombers pass over battered and defenseless England. Who was giving orders to the dictators and the generals?

Next came the Normandy invasion. Here I participated but not in the first wave. The invasion was scheduled on my 27th birthday, June 5, 1944. But again heaven intervened and it was postponed for one day on account of the weather. Somehow I have always looked at this as a personal heavenly favor. I would not want to celebrate my birthday on the day when so many brave men died. I can vividly remember the morning of June 6, 1944. I was in Oldham, England, where the first test-tube baby was born many years later.

All the bells were ringing in triumph. I felt more like crying because I knew that thousands of young men were dying in Normandy at that very moment. On that day not a single German plane or submarine opposed the invasion fleet even though the Germans had thousands in the area. The weather became so bad that no invasion could have been mounted for the next sixty days. The losses were great but Pharaoh's army was defeated on the beaches of France. Israel had made it safely to the other side.

The defeat of the Afrika Korps at the gates of Cairo was perhaps the greatest miracle of all. When we were with Patton on his mad dash across Germany, an infantry captain generously bestowed one hundred and twenty Afrika Korps war prisoners on me. Most of them were top sergeants. I locked them all in a jail in a captured German town and then suddenly remembered that I had forgotten to search them. I returned alone and unarmed and entered the jail where the prisoners were kept in one large area. Never had I seen a tougher or more professional looking group of soldiers. They were the elite of the elite, paratrooper rangers with an average of three years in the African desert campaign. Very politely I announced in German that I was going to search each one for weapons. Any one of them could have killed me with his bare hands. Instead, they all humbly submitted to the search. Perhaps it was helpful that I kept reminding them how lucky they were to have fallen into American rather than Russian hands. When the search was finished, I emerged from the jail with a bushel basket full of Lugers, Walthers, P38s and SS daggers. If I still had them today, they would be worth a small fortune. For a while I was the most popular man in the whole U.S. Army.

It was this kind of professional army that the British faced at the gates of Cairo. The Tommies were brave and competent but terribly outclassed. If Cairo fell, the entire Middle East, including the Bible lands, would be wide open to German invasion. The decisive battle was joined with the odds definitely in favor of the Germans. Suddenly a whole company of Afrika Korps veterans threw down their arms and surrendered. They had broken into a new British water line during the initial three-hour period when it was being tested with salt water. Too late, they tasted the salt and in the 120° heat were forced to surrender immediately. The Lord of battles had again intervened. This time He was protecting Palestine in order that the Jews might return to their homeland. General Montgomery, the British Joshua, must have known that the Lord was on his side. But I don't think that even this brave man of God really knew why.

The final puzzle was Germany's attact on Russia. If Russia had remained neutral and Germany had not been forced into a two-front war, the outcome of World War II would certainly have been different. At first the German armies met with tremendous success in Russia. The oppressed Russian peasants welcomed them as liberators. Then the savage SS took over the newly occupied territories and administered them with even greater than their normal cruelty. Word swept through Russia, that as bad as the Communist leaders were, the Germans were even worse. Stalin managed to unify the nation around the issue of sheer survival, and resistance stiffened tremendously. Hitler made two more fatal mistakes in Russia. He had already started two weeks behind schedule and his armies had to be indoors when the savage Russian winter set in. Then instead of taking Moscow, which he could have had for the asking, Hitler made the fatal mistake of ordering Stalingrad to be taken. The rest is history. God had allowed a self-destructive madness to come upon the German leader. Germany was already being punished for the holocaust. The hand of God's judgment lay heavy upon both Germany and Russia. Stalingrad was the wrath of God raining down upon human sin.

These and other mysteries I pondered in my heart. Then long after the war ended, about six years ago, a Jesuit priest recommended a book entitled, *Rees Howells Intercessor* by Norman Grubb. After I had begun to read I couldn't put it down. Here were the answers to all the major unsolved puzzles of World War II. God was the God of battles after all. He was the Lord of history no matter what men might think. Satan might be the prince of this world, but even he was compelled to obey a regime he couldn't possibly understand or resist. God exercises His sovereignty even in the midst of bullets, bombs and shells. He rules the world not from an ornate altar surrounded by incense, robed clergy and choirs, but from the depths of human tragedy.

Rees Howells was a Welsh coal miner turned evangelist. In 1939 he had a word from the Lord that Hitler would be defeated. This word was published in both the church and secular press. Shortly thereafter Hitler, in spite of the prophecy, proceeded to take over all of Europe. Rees Howells was called a false prophet and a charlatan. But he knew that the Lord had spoken to him. He knew the word was true, and so under the Lord's guidance he determined to make the prophecy self-fulfilling.

All night and nearly every night for five years Rees Howells and his school of intercessors prayed about the war. The Holy Spirit told them what to pray and even let them in on high military secrets. Before a crucial event the Spirit would give them specific directions on what to pray and why. During the final critical phase of the Battle of Britain the Spirit said, "Pray that the Luftwaffe will break off the battle before Britain is defeated and the last base for Western Christendom destroyed." They obeyed and the Luftwaffe veered off just when the last British fighter plane was disabled and on the ground.

During the battle for Cairo the Spirit said, "Pray that the Afrika Korps will be stopped at the Gates of Cairo in order that the Bible lands will be saved." They prayed and the incident with the water line occurred. Before Germany's invasion of Russia the Spirit said, "Pray that Germany will attack Russia because I am going to judge them both." Later the Spirit said, "Pray that the German armies will not take Moscow but will commit suicide in Stalingrad instead." Again and again the Spirit told them what to pray and when they obeyed, the answer came immediately and dramatically. One great lesson that they learned was, "All true prayer is guided prayer." The first prayer is to ask for the prayer. When we pray what we already know to be God's will, the answer is positive and immediate. Rees Howells' intercessors received God's will in an extraordinary way. We normally receive it through His Word. The Word tells us plainly and repeatedly what God's will is. This will is to be carried out through the obedience of prayer.

Rees Howells alone prayed down the Dunkirk evacuation. For three days and three nights he wandered along the beach, caught up in agonized intercession. The sheer burden of it broke him in body and soul. Like Jacob he limped for the rest of his days as a reminder of his close encounter with God. When God wills, a mighty intercession can be carried out by one man. Praying Hyde alone prayed the gospel into India and C. T. Studd into Africa. Intercession is powerful because the intercessor is not alone. He prays with the Father, Son and Holy Spirit and with the whole church on earth and in heaven. God's will plus His time plus the company of heaven still requires one key factor: the obedience of an earthly intercessor. Since the incarnation, God wills not to work without man.

## Chapter 7

# THE INTERCESSOR GOES OUT FROM HIMSELF

The intercessor can ask nothing for himself. He goes out from himself and becomes a hostage to those for whom he prays. A person can be saved and filled with the Spirit, but still be on an ego trip. Intercession is the first going out from oneself. It is the real beginning of the spiritual journey. At the last judgment, according to Matthew 25, Jesus will be looking for His own compassionate nature inside of born-again believers. Because He lives in them they will natural-ly feed the hungry and visit the sick and imprisoned. In fact, this will be so natural that they are surprised when He brings it up. "Lord, when did we see thee hungry . . . or naked . . . when did we see thee sick?" (Matt. 25:37-39).

The new birth has these phases: (1) a new relationship to God, (2) to self, and (3) to the neighbor. The new rela-tionship to God is a total gift from God and so that is no problem. The new relationship to self is difficult because of the flesh. But the new relationship with the neighbor is the most difficult of all because that requires, like intercession, a total going out from the self. The fully born-again Chris-tian is an intercessor. His natural and his spiritual life are no longer focused on self. Compassion is so natural for him that he will be surprised when Jesus says on the last judg-ment, "I was hungry and thirsty and sick and in prison and you ministered to me."

The intercessor prays for God. In the Lord's Prayer we are taught to say, "Hallowed be thy name, thy kingdom come, thy will be done." There is not a single petition that asks to make us good or holy. God wants us to get our minds off ourselves by praying for Him. That's also why Jesus says in Matthew 9:28, "Pray the Lord of the harvest that he will send workers into his harvest." He's the Lord of the harvest and it's His harvest, but He wants us to pray for His work so that we will get our minds off our own goals. The intercessor not only goes out from himself and prays for others, but he also gets his mind off himself and thinks of God. Neopentecostals are often accused of being pharisaical. If there is any truth in this accusation, it is because they have not matured into intercessors. The intercessor is a servant of servants like his master before him.

The intercessor prays with God. According to Romans 8:26-27, the Spirit prays in and with and for us with sighs and groans too deep for words. The Father stands before himself constantly making intercession for the saints according to His will. In Romans 8:34 and Hebrews 7:25, Jesus is at the right hand of the Father constantly making intercession for us. We pray for God and God prays with us; thus the cosmic circle of intercession is complete. All things great and small, temporal and eternal can be drawn into this infinite prayer chain. As we are drawn up into the eternal intercession of God, all evil things within and around us are finally consumed in this plan of divine love.

The intercessor prays with the whole church. Petitionary prayer is a solitary and often a selfish thing. We want God's will to be conformed to our wishes. Our selfish needs have first priority. But no man lives or dies unto himself. God has created us in the solidarity of Adam and redeemed us into the solidarity of Christ. The church is a body and the family is its basic unit. The intercessor understands the powerful reality of the church. He prays with all who believe or have ever believed in Christ. He joins in with the ten thousand times ten thousand and the whole company of heaven to celebrate one Lord, one faith, one baptism, and one God and Father of all. Because the intercessor prays with God and with His whole church, nothing can resist His prayer. It is the unanimous vote of heaven and earth that God's will be done.

When this great power of intercession is focused on the family, something has to happen. Here two prayer covenants come together and reinforce each other. God wants us to be intercessors for His will and He wants our entire households to be saved.

## Chapter 8

# THE COVENANT

*Heavenly Father, you have made us for yourself and we cannot rest until we rest in you. We believe that no man can come to you on his own. He must be brought by the Spirit. We believe that all evangelism is prayer and that everyone is prayed into the kingdom. Forgive us for making up our own religion and for trying to beat a path to your door. Help us to understand the puzzling mysteries of covenant and calling. Father, it's so hard to believe that we are loved for nothing; we desperately need to feel some kind of worthiness. Holy Spirit, stir up our hearts to respond to the God who is already here. Show us that all true worship is a breakthrough from the other side. We thank you, Father, Son and Holy Spirit, that you have chosen us before the foundation of the world. Let that eternal covenant never be broken. Let us never take you or our calling for granted but eternally celebrate your covenant of amazing grace.*

*In Jesus' Name. Amen.*

The Bible is a covenant book from cover to cover. In the New Testament there are two basic Greek words for covenant: *diatheke* and *syntheke*. "Diatheke" is a unilateral declaration of intent. It is God telling us in advance exactly how He is going to deal with us. There are no negotiations or consultations; the vehicle and the final decision are totally God's. For this reason "diatheke" is often translated by will or testament. From this we get the Old and the New

Testament, which simply mean God's old and new covenant with us.

"Syntheke," on the other hand, is an agreement between two parties that is mutually negotiated. This implies
some degree of equality. "Syntheke" requires certain qualifications from the second party before it can be consum-
mated. All God's covenants with us are "diatheke." The
qualifications and the variables are all in Him. In John
6:65, Jesus says, "No one can come to me unless it is
granted him by the Father." In John 15:16, He says, "You
did not choose me, but I chose you." The relationship of
this covenant is unequal in terms of what each partner
brings and contributes. The biblical covenant is a one-way
street in which man's only function is to respond to what
has already been done for him.

Baptism and circumcision are "diatheke" covenants.
For this reason they can also be concluded with infants.
God sets the terms and He alone pays the full price. When
Jesus instituted the Last Supper He said, "This is the new
covenant in my blood," or "this is my blood of the covenant" (Matt. 26:28; Mark 14:24; 1 Cor. 11:25; Ex. 24:8;
Zech. 9:11; Heb. 12:20). The covenant of forgiveness and
salvation can be made with sinful man only because God in
Christ paid the price of blood. Again and again God rein-
forces the covenant by the most sacred of all oaths, "As I
live, says the Lord." Because God alone makes the covenant and also paid the price and then swears to it by His
own life, the covenant is the most sacred and sure promise
of all eternity (Ps. 89:34). It is an everlasting covenant
(Gen. 17:3, 7, 19; Lev. 24:8; Isa. 24:5, 61:8; Ps. 105:10; Ezek.
37:26; Jer. 32:40; 1 Chron. 16:17; and 1 Sam. 23:5).

God's covenant is sacred and unbreakable. Such was
the covenant made with Noah, Abraham, Jacob and David.
So sacred before the Lord is the covenant that even a hu-

man covenant made through deceit is considered unbreakable. In Joshua 9 we read how Joshua was tricked into making a sacred covenant with the Gibeonites. By coming with
worn clothing and moldy food the Gibeonites deceived
Joshua into believing that they came from far away. Then
we read in 2 Samual 21 that 400 years later there was a
three-year famine in Israel. When David asked the Lord
why, he was told there was a blood guilt on Saul and his
house because he broke the covenant with the Gibeonites.
Seven sons of Saul were hanged to expiate that guilt. As far
as God is concerned, a sworn covenant can never be reversed even though it is based upon deceit.

The covenant is a covenant of life and salvation. In
Ezekiel 18:23, the Lord says, "Have I any pleasure in the
death of the wicked . . . and not rather that he should turn
from his way and live?" In 1 Timothy 2:4, Paul says that
God wants all men to be saved and to come to the knowledge of the truth. It's a covenant of peace and not of warfare. In 1 Timothy 2:2, Paul says that God wants us to lead
quiet and peaceable lives. In Isaiah 52:7 and 57:19, God
speaks about a covenant of peace.

The basic unit of the covenant is the human family.
Throughout the Bible the covenant is made with families
and households. It is not the nation or the individual but
the family to whom God gives His covenant promises. The
primary biblical covenants were concluded with Noah,
Abraham and David. The most important family covenant
of all was made with Mary in Luke 2.

In the following chapters the biblical solidarity of the
human family will be traced. Here we shall see that God indeed sets the solitary in families. God in Christ entered human history through an ordinary human family. The promises and the honor given to Mary in Luke 2 emphasizes the
sacredness of the personal family covenant which God

makes with the mother of Jesus. When Christ was hanging on the cross, with the weight of the world's sins on His back and with death staring Him in the face, He concluded His Jewish covenant relationship with His mother. "Woman, behold thy son, and son, behold thy mother" was a sacred family bond that no pious Jew could ignore.

God himself makes the covenant. He himself pays the price. It is sacred, eternal and unbreakable. The primary unit of the divine covenant is the human family.

## Chapter 9

# HE SETS THE SOLITARY IN FAMILIES

*Heavenly Father, you have made us for yourself and each other. Help us to overcome the feelings of loneliness and isolation. Destroy in us the alienation of sin. Father, help us to understand that we are not rugged individualists responsible only to ourselves, but eternal members of a larger body. Forgive our self-centeredness and our selfish living. Give us a vision of that physical and spiritual unity in which you have placed us. Let the Holy Spirit guide us to make every prayer a family covenant prayer. Change the "I" to "we" and let us always see ourselves as members of the family into which God has placed us. Forgive our blindness, our anger and resentments which work against family unity. Lord Jesus, show us that we are a real part of you and each other.*

*In Jesus' Name. Amen.*

According to Romans 5 and 6, the human race consists of only two people: Adam and Christ. The American ideal of the rugged individualist is not biblical. "None of us lives to himself, and none of us dies to himself" (Rom. 14:7). God deals with us primarily as family units. The tribes of Israel, upon which the church was founded, were families. The genealogy of Jesus in Matthew and Luke shows God's concern with families. On the human side, Jesus did not simply come from nowhere; He came in the human family. Thirty years of His earthly life were spent in a simple family setting in Nazareth. God became a real part of us by being born into a human family.

In the thinking of the Bible, the family is presented as a kind of corporate personality. In order to understand the biblical texts clearly, we must free ourselves of our modern individualistic thinking. The biblical concept of family represents a unity represented by the father of the household. All important questions were decided by the father, and his decisions were binding upon all the members of the household. This was particularly true of decisions relating to God. In the ancient mind the faith of the father of the household was decisive. He decided what religion the whole family would follow. His covenant with God was binding on the whole family. God's promises to him included his whole household.

According to Joachim Jeremias in *The Origins of Infant Baptism* (SCM Press, LTD, London, 1963), the Old Testament uses "house" (Bayit) in the place of family. This is an all-inclusive term, especially when the word "kol" (whole) is added. Some references are: (he or she) "You and your whole house" (house of your father) (Gen. 7:1, 36:6, 45:8, 50:7f., 47:12; Deut. 6:22; 1 Sam. 1:21, 22:15, 9:20, 22:16, 22:1; 2 Sam. 6:11, 6:21, 9:9; Josh. 2:18; Judges 16:31).

There are some seventy-three Old Testament passages that convey the solidarity of the human family. This has a negative as well as a positive result. The father of the family eats a meal, changes houses, seeks refuge, is blessed, saved, stricken with plagues, annihilated, burned and killed with all his household. These things are received, done or suffered by all the members of the family without exception. These passages indicate that in the view of God, the family is not merely a temporary collection of individuals, but a permanent corporate unit. This solidarity is reflected in the Apochryphal books and in Rabinic Judaism. It is also to be found in the Rabinic tradition concerning the baptism of proselytes. According to Alfred Edersheim's book, *The Life and Times of Jesus the Messiah*, whole families of proselytes were commonly baptized into Judaism before and during the time of Christ. Families were taken into the covenant as units—parents and children, including infants.

According to Jeremias' *Infant Baptism in the First Four Centuries* (SCM Press, London, 1964, p. 23), the unbaptized members of the household were excluded from the table fellowship of the family. Because the religious solidarity of the family was assumed, it was unthinkable that any member of the household would not be baptized if the head of the household was.

The apostolic church also baptized whole families like those of Cornelius, the Philippian jailor and Stephanas in Corinth. The New Testament repeatedly mentions that "households" are devout (Acts 10:2), receive salvation (Acts 11:14; 16:31), become believers (John 4:53, Acts 18:8) and are baptized (1 Cor. 1:16; 16:15). In the case of the jailor of Philippi (Acts 16:31-33), it is mentioned three times that the family was complete (Jeremias, pp. 22, 23).

Sometimes, as in the case of Crispus, the father seems to act alone for the whole family. In Acts 18:8, Paul says that Crispus became a believer with all of his household. Yet in 1 Corinthians 1:14, Paul says that he baptized Crispus alone without mentioning his house. In one case a woman, Lydia, is mentioned as the head of the household (Acts 16:15). This shows that family solidarity was not simply a matter of the patriarchal priesthood of the father.

Kittel's Theological Dictionary of the New Testament (Kolhammer, Stuttgart, Vol. I, p. 33, German), summarizes the biblical use of the word "house" or "household." Family is the smallest natural entity in the Christian congregations. The New Testament church was built around the family household. The bishops are first of all to rule well in their own households (1 Tim. 3:4). The deacons are to provide for their households (1 Tim. 3:12). The false teachers mislead households (2 Tim. 1:16; 4:19). In the primitive church bread was broken from house to house, the word was taught and gospel proclaimed from house to house (Acts 2:46; 5:42). Again and again it is emphasized that the conversion of the father brings the whole household to faith. In Acts 20:20, Paul defends what he taught openly in the houses. Thus the New Testament church was a house church and the family was the basic unit of the new covenant as well as the old.

According to Kittel (Vol. VII, p. 1070, English), the Apostle Paul does not see any direct individual fellowship of man with Christ; only that of the community or of the individual member within the community (1 Cor. 10:16). When the individual cleaves to the Lord, he is in the Spirit. The body of Christ is the community, never the individual. Paul is here trying to rule out individual mysticism. Because Christ is a body here on earth and we are a real part of that body, everything we do, including fornication, involves Him (1 Cor. 6:15). The physical connection with Christ and the members of His body is real but not tangible. On the other hand, the physical and other links in the family are obvious.

Paul describes the church as a real physical body in 1 Corinthians 12. On the Damascus Road he saw that Christ and all believers were one. When Jesus said, "Why are you persecuting me?" Paul did not argue that he was only persecuting the deluded followers of Jesus (Acts 9:4-5). When Paul describes the church as the body of Christ, he is not using a metaphor or a simile; he is describing what he actually saw with his own two eyes there on the Damascus Road.

In the Old Testament the father is the priest in his family. This means that the religious covenants are made by him alone. He offers up the sacrifices and mediates between his family and God. He is also the intercessor who speaks for his household before the Lord. In the new covenant this function of the father continues but now focuses on baptism and worship rather than circumcision and sacrifice. In 1 Timothy 8-15 Paul talks about intercession in the context of the relationship between men and women in the church. The fathers as intercessors are to lift up holy hands without wrath and quarreling. They are the intercessors and not the accusers or judges for their families. Satan is the accuser and if the father does not act as intercessor, the family has no one to represent it before the Lord.

Because the father is its priest and the family is a spiritual unit, the prayers of the family are always corporate prayers. When we pray in the family setting, we should not see ourselves as individuals in strife and competition but as one body before the Lord. In 1 Peter 3:7 we read that husbands should honor their wives as fellow heirs of the grace of life in order that their prayers not be hindered. When husbands and wives see themselves as competing separate individuals, their prayers may shoot each other down like anti-aircraft guns. In a divided household the prayers are often prayers against each other. Like birds with broken wings, these fractured prayers never quite get off the ground.

## SOLIDARITY IN DEATH

Dr. Kuebler-Ross of Chicago and Dr. Raymond A. Moody Jr. have reported on the phenomenon of family solidarity at the time of death. Dr. Moody, M.D. Phd., is both a psychiatrist and a philosopher. His books *Life After Life* and *Reflections on Life After Life* (Bantam 1977) clearly indicate that the solidarity of the human family is also manifested in the hour of death. He reports incident after incident when family members come to meet the dying to escort them to the other side. This is further substantiated by Archie Matson in his book, *Afterlife* (Harper & Row 1975). An exhaustive scientific study of the subject of dying is to be found in the book *At the Hour of Death* by Karlis Osis and Erlendur Haraldsson (Avon, 1977). Case after case is reported in which the dying encounter relatives about whose recent death they had not been informed. The most common encounters are with immediate family members who are involved in 90% of all death-bed apparitions.

This compared closely to my own experiences as a hospital chaplain when I attended as many as a thousand deaths. Many times I heard the dying patient greeting long dead relatives. In Libby, Montana, a 91-year-old woman, who died on Easter Sunday, frequently reported seeing her deceased parents and grandparents. I visited her every day during Holy Week and she related to me the vivid dreams she had about departed members of the family. This is a phenomenon of death that seems to occur in a majority of cases when clear observation of the dying is possible. Whatever the role of the family in eternity may be, its function extends into the very hour of death itself. There is no doubt that the solidarity of the human family transcends mere biology. There is a spiritual unity that is greater than genes.

This solidarity of the family can bring both blessing and bondage. Many times the Bible mentions that people are blessed because of their forefathers. This is especially true in the case of David's descendants (1 Kings 5:7, 9:4, 11:12, 11:32-33, 11:36, 15:3; 2 Kings 8:19, 19:34, 20:6). The Hebrew word *dor* and the Greek word *genea* express this idea through the English translation "generation." God blesses and curses; He promises and He covenants through the generations of men. The curse is only as deep as the third or fourth generation, while the covenant blessing lasts for a thousand (Deut. 7:9).

This solidarity of guilt results in what is called "Bondage of the Generations." Clergymen, social workers and mental health professors have long known that trouble comes in family bunches like bananas. There is a clustering of difficulties not fully explainable by genetic and sociological contagions. There are destructive patterns that seem to repeat themselves compulsively generation after generation. This suggests an ancestral bondage of guilt that must somehow be dealt with.

The family covenant is not only positive but to some degree also negative. There is a solidarity of guilt and grace with grace far outweighing guilt. In the Old Testament guilt remains for only three or four generations, while blessing endures for a thousand (Deut. 5:9-10). Moreover, ancestral bondage can be dealt with once we become aware of it. Sometimes it is indeed the secret key to a whole succession of family problems that seem to have no rational basis. The book *Demon Possession*, edited by John Warwick Montgomery, suggests a way of dealing with ancestral bondage:

> An elderly Canon of the Anglican church became quite terrified when he found himself appointed as official exorcist for the diocese. He asked for help. I asked why and he replied: "My daughter is locked in a padded cell in a mental hospital, and there is nothing they can do to help her." Her main trouble was that she had an overwhelming urge to gouge out the eyes of her children. I remarked that this seemed a very primitive form of behavior and inquired who her ancestors were. He informed me that her mother, his wife, was a titled lady from an ancient castle. I knew from having visited this castle that at one time this form of torture had been practiced there. The present family apparently never went near the place and knew nothing of it. I suggested to the Canon that he should see his bishop and

ask his advice. The bishop said that we should have a Eucharist of remembrance and that he would be free in five days' time to celebrate this with the two of us. From the moment he made this promise, the Canon's daughter became perfectly normal. A few days later we heard that her aunt who was unknown to me in another mental hospital had been cured at the same time. Neither of these two knew anything of the conversation with the bishop. The Canon, too, was released from his anxieties and has helped many others since then.

A similar case is reported on pages 275, 276 of the same book:

> For seven years a young nun's acute bouts of disruptive behavior had shattered the peace of the closed community to which she belonged. I asked her to draw a family tree and this she was able to do. It showed clearly a repeated pattern of behavior. I was asked to speak to the nunnery on the subject of Satan's use of this family pattern to destroy and disrupt. Forty nuns produced similar problems, including family suicides, mental breakdowns, disrupted relationships and sudden deaths. With the two chaplains we designed a service which began with praise, then exorcism, confession and absolution. This was followed by their bringing to the altar steps paper on which was written all the problems raised, including the names of the departed; the papers were laid on the altar. Finally there was a shortened service of the Eucharist and, for those who wished, the laying on of hands and holy unction at the altar. The effect on many of the participants' lives was dramatic, both in the order and beyond the nunnery.
>
> In conditions of this type, where exorcism seems indicated, study of the family tree often reveals repeated patterns related to the position of those afflicted: For example, the eldest daughter of seven succeeding generations; the eldest male of each family; the youngest, weakest person at the time of onset.

About a year ago a family came to me at North Heights because they were having extreme difficulty integrating two adopted daughters into their household. The adopted sisters came from an extremely degraded moral background into a middle class, professional Christian family. We prayed for release from ancestral bondage and I anointed the entire family with oil. When I laid hands on the two girls, they were immediately slain in the Spirit and remained unconscious for ten or fifteen minutes. After they had regained consciousness, the bondage of guilt seemed to have been broken. Subsequently, they were able to make a completely new adjustment into the adoptive family. In other instances lifelong Christians were released from mysterious oppression in this manner. In some cases the releasing ministry assumed the form of deliverance.

Destructive family patterns are often repeated from generation to generation. There appears to be a highly compulsive reinactment by each generation of the deepest moral and spiritual conflicts of the preceding generations. Alcoholism, suicide and violence are the most common destructive patterns which appear again and again on the family tree. Sometimes the pattern is related to the family position of those affected, for example, the eldest male or the eldest daughter or the youngest, weakest person. There are many dimensions through which our ancestors influence us, but by far the most subtle and powerful is the spiritual. Alex Haley's powerful book *Roots* has started a new trend. We all need to have a closer look at our family trees if we do not wish to pass destructive and defeating patterns on to future generations.

## Chapter 10

# THE NEW COVENANT OF SPIRIT

In the Old Testament there was another kind of ancestral bondage. The iniquities of the fathers were visited on the children to the third and fourth generation (Ex. 34:7; Lev. 20:9; Num. 14:18). We see this happening immediately and directly in the families of Korah (Num. 16:31-32) and the persecutors of Daniel (6:24). The whole household of Korah was swallowed up by the earth and taken alive to Sheol because Korah had rebelled against Moses. The entire families of those who had caused Daniel to be placed into the lions' den were thrown to the lions themselves. In the case of Achan (Judges 7:22-25), his whole family was stoned and all his possessions burned because he had hidden in his tent some of the spoils taken from the battle.

This kind of ancestral guilt and punishment seems very shocking to us, but the ancient world accepted it without question. The pagan world expected the sins of the fathers to be visited upon their children. This is the theme of the famous Greek play, "Oedipus Rex," by Euripedes. The more primitive a society is, the greater its sense of unity. Individualism is a product of a highly differentiated technical society. In the new covenant of the Spirit, God clearly defines the nature and scope of His covenant with man. It still focuses on the family, but the solidarity of guilt has been replaced by the solidarity of grace.

In Jeremiah 31:29-34, the prophet describes the new covenant of Spirit which God will make with Israel and the church. "No longer shall they say, The fathers have eaten sour grapes and the children's teeth are set on edge, but each one shall be responsible for his own sin." The new covenant is not one of law and judgment but an internal transformation of the individual through the power of the Holy Spirit. It is eternal, unbreakable and covers all the descendants of Israel.

The new covenant is further clarified in Joel 2:28-29, "I will pour out my Spirit upon all flesh." The terms "sons and daughters, young men and old men, manservants and maidservants" are idioms for "whole household." The children are not coming generations only but the sons and daughters of those present. In Acts 2:39, "the promise is unto you and your children" refers not only to the descendants of the listeners but also to their covenant households. Because Peter and the other apostles apparently expected the immediate return of Christ, they did not believe that they or their hearers would have any more descendants.

First Corinthians 7:14 is a direct testimony to the family covenant. Here Paul says that the unbelieving wife or husband is sanctified by the mere fact of living with a believing mate. In the same way the children are not unclean but holy because they are descended from a believing parent. Thus the products of a mixed marriage are not ceremonially impure in Jewish thinking because one believing member sanctifies the whole household. This is one of the most tremendous passages on marriage in the entire New Testament; yet most of the time it has only been used to justify desertion as a legitimate ground for divorce. This holiness of the children in this mixed Christian-heathen marriage rests not on baptism, which they would scarcely have agreed upon, but soley on descent from a Christian father or mother.

In Mark 10:13-16, Jesus sharply rejects the idea that children are not a real part of the kingdom covenant. It was a Jewish custom to bring all the children to be blessed by a scribe on the Day of Atonement. Through this the parents hoped that they might attain knowledge of the Torah and of good works. The disciples apparently believed that Jesus would not want to continue this kind of tradition. Jesus' reply, "Let them come and don't keep them away," shows that they had an immediate share in the coming kingdom because they belonged to covenant households. In fact, the kingdom is made up of households that include infants: "For of such is the kingdom of God."

The New Testament says that "households" are devout (Acts 10:2), receive salvation (Acts 11:14, 16:31), become believers (John 4:53; Acts 18:8) and are baptized (1 Cor. 1:16; Acts 16:15). Sometimes the term "whole" or "entire" is used to signify that no single member of the household is left out. The household in the narrower sense includes the father, the mother, and all the children. In the wider sense it includes all the relatives living in the house (Joachim Jeremias, *The Origins of Infant Baptism* SCM Press London, 1963 p. 12).

The external sign of the family covenant is water baptism. In the book of Acts there are only two instances of an individual being baptized alone. Both of these were very extraordinary circumstances: the Apostle Paul in Acts 9 and the Ethiopian eunuch in Acts 8. Most of the instances recorded were family groups or households. In the early apostolic church, households were taken into the Christian fellowship through baptism. This usually happened on Easter Sunday morning. It was necessary because according to the Pseudo-Clementine writings, no Christian could, under any circumstances, sit at table with a pagan. This included father, mother, wife, child, brother and other relatives. The rule went back to the Jewish prohibition about eating with pagans (Jeremias, op. cit., p. 28 ff.).

According to Jeremias (op. cit., p. 83 ff.), baptism is not *merely a bath of cleansing*, but is also the crossing of the *waters into safety:* 1 Cor. 10:1; 1 Pet. 3:19-21.

It is an action that *saves from perdition:* Acts 2:40, 16:30; Eph. 2:5, 8; 1 Pet. 3:20.

It is a *change of lordship:* Col. 1:13; Rom. 6:1-11; Eph. 2:5; Col. 2:12, 20; Col. 3:1.

It *mediates the Spirit:* Acts 1:5, 2:38, 9:17, 11:16, 19:5; 1 Cor. 12:13; 2 Cor. 1:22.

It is *a new creation:* 2 Cor. 5:17; Gal. 6:15.

It is *being born anew:* Jer. 3:5; Titus 3:5; 1 Pet. 1:3, 23; 2:2.

It is *incorporation* into the *body of Christ:* 2 Cor. 1:22; Eph. 1:13; 4:30; 1 Cor. 12:13.

It is *union with God's people:* Eph. 2:12, 19.

It is *God's covenant through Christian circumcision:* Col. 2:11.

It is *imparting the inheritance and the life:* Gal. 3:29; Titus 3:7; 1 Pet. 1:4; Col. 3:3.

It is the *divine act of justification, adoption, sanctification, enlightenment* and *putting on Christ:* 1 Cor. 6:11; Gal. 3:26; Rom. 8:15; Gal. 4:6; 1 Cor. 6:11; Heb. 6:4, 10:32; Gal. 3:27; Col. 2:11.

The family covenant is mediated and supported by the powerful list of baptismal promises. In all there are over fifty passages listing the baptismal covenants. They do not speak about an age of other limits. They are given to a people who regarded it as normal to be admitted to God's covenant through circumcision on the eighth day and who looked upon baptism as the circumcision of Christ and the seal of God. Water baptism is the sign and the seal of our incorporation into God's family covenant.

In the New Testament, baptismal grace is experienced as a total thing. Anything which isolates individual aspects,

such as forgiveness of sins or bestowal of the Spirit, over-
looks the wholeness of the New Testament theology of baptism. This same wholeness of thinking also applies to the
Christian community and their families. The whole people
of God were baptized when they passed through the Red
Sea (1 Cor. 10:1 f.). The whole family of Noah was saved in
the ark, symbolizing baptism (1 Pet. 3:20 f.). The promise of
the Spirit is referred to the houses (to you and your children) in Acts 2:39. They are seen as one unit in the sight of
God. The faith of the father of the house as representing the
family, along with the faith of the mother, embraces the
children as well. The universal character of Christ's grace
reveals itself in that it is the "houses" which are summoned
to believe and be baptized (Joachim Jeremias, op. cit., pp.
84, 85).

The implications and the practical application of all of
this are very clear. If we cannot save our loved ones by witness and admonition, then we can certainly claim them in
family covenant intercession. Often our witness and admonition are counterproductive because of conflicts in the relationship. When this happens, then a silent claiming of the
family covenant of water and the Spirit must take over. But
first of all we need to stop looking at spirit, salvation and
baptism as merely individual gifts. When we begin to see
these as family covenant, then every individual prayer is
automatically turned into a family covenant prayer.

In Mark 10:13 we have the account of the children being
brought to Jesus for blessing. This was a Jewish custom in
Jerusalem on the Day of Atonement. Those who were a year
old were brought until daybreak and the twelve-year-olds
until evening. They were brought to the elders and scribes
for prayer and blessing in order that they might one day attain to the knowledge of the Torah and good works. Jesus'
acceptance and blessing of the children showed that they

were a very real part of the spiritual covenants entered into by their parents. The blessings of the kingdom belonged to them also because they were a part of the covenant households.

## THE WHOLENESS OF SALVATION

The Greek word *soteria* is used for salvation in the New Testament. The verb *sozein* means to save. In classical Greek, "soteria" means deliverance or preservation. It can mean a safe return from a journey or security against danger. In the papyri, the commonest meaning was bodily health. In classical Greek correspondence, members of the family would routinely inquire about each other's "soteria." In intertestimental period "soteria" means safety, security and deliverance from trouble or an enemy. It is used to describe Israel's deliverance from the Red Sea. In general "soteria" is the kind of help and deliverance that only God can give.

In New Testament Greek "soteria" is used of bodily health and safety. It describes Paul's preservation in shipwreck (Acts 27:20, 34). It also describes Naoh's building the ark to save himself and his family (Heb. 11:7). The verb "sozein" means to save a man in the eternal sense and to heal a man in the physical sense. Salvation in the New Testament is total; it saves a man's body, soul and spirit for time and eternity.

"SOTERIA" is *salvation from physical illness:* Matt. 7:21; Luke 8:36.

It is *salvation from danger.* When the disciples were in peril, they cried out to be saved: Matt. 8:25; 14:30.

It is *salvation from life's infection.* A man is saved from a crooked and perverse generation: Acts 2:40.

It is *salvation from lostness.* Jesus came to seek and to save the lost: Matt. 18:11; Luke 19:10.

It is *salvation from sin and wrath:* Matt. 1:21; Rom. 5:9.

But salvation also has a strong *eschatological dimension.* That means we may begin to reap its benefits here, but it will be fully realized only when Jesus is enthroned king of all the world (Rom. 13:11; 1 Cor. 5:5; 2 Tim. 4:18; Heb. 9:28; 1 Pet. 1:5; Rev. 12:10). Finally, *SOTERIA is that which saves a man from all that would ruin him in this life and the life to come* (Adopted from William Barclay, New Testament Words, Westminster, Philadelphia, 1974).

Salvation is all inclusive and also corporate. We are saved body, soul and spirit for time and eternity not just as individuals but as whole households. There is no individual in the family who is not included in this vast spectrum of rescue. God is like a fireman who not only rescues us from the burning building but also our family and all our belongings. When Jesus healed, He never healed just one member or one part of the body. Similarly, when He offers salvation, it is not just to one family member but to the whole body.

One night I was presenting this material to a Bible study class at North Heights Lutheran Church. A family of four adults sat right in front of me drinking it all in. As they left the church that night they were praying the family covenant prayer together. With new insight they began to pray in unison for the total salvation of their household. It was a cold and snowy night and as they pulled onto Rice Street, which runs in front of North Heights, they were struck from the rear by a truck. This car turned over some four times and was totaled, but none of the family received more than a scratch. As they were praying the family covenant prayer together, it seemed as if the Lord wrapped their whole family in a giant protective cocoon. This was an immediate sign confirming the word they had just received.

## Chapter 11

# PRAYING THE FAMILY COVENANT

At the 1978 International Lutheran Conference on the Holy Spirit, Father Francis McNutt and I conducted a joint healing workshop. Fr. McNutt managed to convince me that he and I were really bottlenecks in the healing ministry of the church. Our job was to show others how to claim the healing power of God for themselves. One technique that he taught me has been especially helpful. This involves getting husband and wife and/or family members to lay hands on the backs of each other's necks and to regularly pray for each other up to 30 minutes per day. I have adopted that to the family covenant and found it especially helpful in marriage counseling.

Sometimes the couples who come into our counseling center are very hostile. Many of them are Roman Catholics who have come to hate one another and are only held together by the discipline and sanctions of the church. In many cases these couples have teenagers who are in open and highly destructive rebellion. Praying the family covenant daily by laying hands on each other symbolizes the sacramental unity that God has created in the biological family. The sacramental act of family covenant prayer is a spiritual fountain out of which healing and love can flow to every member. This kind of prayer closes ranks so that Satan can no longer attack and harass at will.

There are many ways to pray the family covenant—alone or together. Since August of 1976, when I spoke on the family covenant at the International Conference on the

Holy Spirit in Minneapolis, I have received hundreds of testimonies. Several were about little old ladies in wheelchairs who quietly prayed all their relatives into the kingdom. One such grandmother began to pray when she was confined to a wheelchair at 65 and continued to claim the covenant every waking hour until she died at 95. She prayed her whole relationship, down to third cousins, into the kingdom! All the time that she was doing it no one paid any attention to her. They thought she was just a senile old grandmother waiting for death.

The family covenant prayers that seems to be most effective are those prayed by mothers for their children. Mothers are like Mary, "God bearers." They are the first evangelists. From them we hear the first word of God and learn our first prayer. From them we first learn the meaning of love, trust and sacrifice. Women who bear the greater share of responsibility for the Fall, have also been compensated with a deeper spirituality. Mary, the second Eve, stood beneath the tree of the cross and offered up her divine Son for the sin of the first Eve beneath another tree. Women pay the greatest penalty for man's cruelty and greed. Again and again, they must offer up the fruit of their bodies on the altar of the god of war. Their hearts are broken and their eyes are often drowned in tears. They can better understand the broken heart of God on the cross. Mothers and wives are the best intercessors because they love more and hurt more. A mother prayed me through the war and into the kingdom. She didn't even know then what the family covenant was, but she knew how to pray it.

In the family covenant prayer I have found an answer to the agonizing cry of mothers who come to me about their husbands and children. Hundreds of times in counseling and ministry the question has been sobbed, "What can I do about my husband (or wife or son or daughter)? Nothing

66

seems to work." Counseling is for people who want help in
changing themselves. Ministry is for those who desire God's
help in doing it. Intercession is for all others. Intercession is
for those who will not seek God's or man's help for themselves. It is for those too blind to see, too stubborn to re-
pent, and too proud to surrender. Intercessions is not meant
to destroy freedom or force repentance but to touch that
deepest chord inside of every miserable prodigal. Only the
Spirit can find that part of us that never cares to long for
God.

Husbands and wives are the best family covenant
prayer team. They are in the covenant of marriage according to Ephesians 5. Because their relationship is like Christ
and the church, they represent the microcosm of the
church. Husbands and wives in Christ are the irreducible
minimum of the Body of Christ. They are the basic core of
intercession. When they come together in the name of
Christ—with Christ present and agree perfectly—they
make God the Father an offer that He cannot refuse (Matt.
18:19-20).

The family covenant prayer seems to work best of all
when it is meaningfully plugged into Christ's body, the
Church. At Trinity in Joppatown, Maryland, we prayed it
with various family units every Wednesday night. Sometimes we managed to pray incoming family members to the
altar in three months' time. Many a time a sheepish husband would come to me and say, "Pastor, I don't really
know what I'm doing here, but I have a feeling that this is
where I'm supposed to be. Pray for me that God would do
whatever He wants with my life."

The greatest secret of the family covenant prayer is per-
sistence. "Take no rest and give him no rest. . . . The Lord
has sworn by his right hand and by his mighty arm" (Isa.
62:6-7). "Cry aloud to the Lord. . . let tears stream down

like a torrent day and night! Give yourself no rest, your eyes no respite! Arise, cry out in the night . . . pour out your heart like water before the presence of the Lord! Lift your hands to him for the lives of your children" (Lam. 2:18-19). "I am weary with my moaning; every night I flood my bed with tears; I drench my couch with my weeping. My eye wastes away because of grief" (Ps. 6:6-7). Can we dare care less than God? The family covenant prayer is an intense prayer, prayed with a broken heart and weeping eyes. It is a cry that goes up day and night.

The family covenant prayer is not an easy way off the hook in family relations. God often requires painful confrontations and changes. We are in part expected to be answers to our own prayers. A mother in Maryland came to me about her family. We prayed the family covenant together each week. Almost every time there would be a new word from the Lord. Sometimes it was more than a mere word of revelation. Events began to call for decisions and action on the part of family members.

"Pastor, my daughter is suddenly beginning to say to me that I never really loved her. What should I do now?"

"Ask her for forgiveness and understanding. Don't be defensive. Be reconciled to your daughter. The Lord is speaking to you in answer to our prayer."

One week she came to me and said, "You know I believe that I have never forgiven my mother for what she said to me once."

"Then go and forgive her. Ask the Lord to search all of your family relationships to see if there are hidden blocks or open doors where Satan might be getting in."

The family covenant prayer is a working through of all the emotional garbage that has accumulated in families for years. The prayer opens up a whole new way of looking at ourselves and each other. God begins to reveal the many ways that we have been hurting ourselves and each other for years.

The family covenant prayer can sometimes be dangerous, too. If we plead with God to save a loved one, He may have to bring about a painful breaking in order to answer the prayer. If the loved one has a serious problem like alcoholism, the Lord may have to bring him to the brink of disaster in order to get his attention. Once a husband in a congregation I was serving screamed at his wife, "Will you stop praying that family covenant over me! I'm getting clobbered. When I'm ready to be saved, I'll let you know."

## Chapter 12

# FAMILY COVENANT PRAYERS

*Heavenly Father, we are bound by time, but every day is as a thousand years and a thousand years as one day with you. Teach us to live in the light of eternity. Teach us to get our priorities in order so that we may always be aware of the promise of full salvation. You see me and my family as one eternal unit before you. Help me to understand this and always to pray with this in mind. Free me from any unknown ancestral bondage. Release me from the solidarity of guilt handed down by birth. If my fathers have eaten sour grapes, don't let my teeth be set on edge. Let my prayers reach and teach those family members who will not and cannot pray for themselves. As all my family members are present before you in this eternal moment, so let my prayers for them come before you and be acceptable unto you.*

*In Jesus' Name. Amen.*

*Heavenly Father, you have said and sworn that you want all men to be saved. You have sworn by your own life that you do not desire the death of the wicked. You have also said that you want all men to be led to salvation through our intercession. By the Holy Spirit give us the power to understand and obey this command in order that we might pray people into the kingdom. Your command and promise especially refer to the members of our families. Let your will to save all men and your promise to save the members of my household now be done on earth as it is done in heaven. Use my prayers as a channel for your holy perfect will.*

Use my intercession as a means to reach and to cover every member of my household. I claim your holy will and promise for all men and especially for the members of my own household.

*In Jesus' Name. Amen.*

Heavenly Father, it's so easy to just stand behind the lines and pray. Make me an answer to my own prayers. Let me be used to carry out the things for which I am praying. Make me sensitive to others' needs and hurts, always willing to do what the Spirit suggests. Holy Spirit, give me the prayers to pray and the will to do and hear. Let my prayers be self-fulfilling prophecies. If you say I must humble myself and forgive, if you say I must first change, let me be obedient. Jesus, do not let me be a stumbling block to my loved ones. Don't let my lack of love keep them from seeing and knowing your perfect love. Put me aside so that you can be made flesh in my own life and family. Let me seek to be Christ to them. Let them always be able to see you in me.

*In Jesus' Name. Amen.*

Heavenly Father, the children you have given me will always be bone of my bone and flesh of my flesh. Nothing can ever change that. How can I be fully saved if even one of them is lost? Teach me to claim their salvation as a vital part of my own. Let me give you and myself no rest day and night but pour out my heart like water before you. You have promised to save my loved ones. You have sworn it in your own faithfulness and you cannot lie. Let me never, never, even for a moment, forget the promise, "I will save you and your household." Father, forgive me for ever doubting this word. Forgive me for despairing over the salvation of my loved ones. Pour the peace of the Holy Spirit over this family. Jesus, as you have in your own body made us eternally one with God, so make the members of my body eternally yours.

*In Your Name. Amen.*

Heavenly Father, save my family whatever the cost might be for me or them. Do whatever you have to do to get their attention. Break every idol and every proud and stubborn will that stands in the way of your eternal promise for us. Father, I offer up myself. I lay my life on the altar before you. Tell me what you want of me. Tell me what is blocking the salvation of my loved ones. Show me what I have to do and pray. Let me not be afraid and pull back if your will for salvation proves costly and dangerous. I pray against the devil and all his works and all his ways. I claim the authority of the new man over the elemental spirits of the universe. Jesus, by the power of your cross and your victory, overcome every resistance on heaven and earth. Holy Spirit, let salvation come to this household today!

*In Your Name. Amen.*

Heavenly Father, we confess that we do not love enough. Give us your own love in Jesus that only desires good for others. Let the burning love of the cross kindle our prayers and cause us to claim, without ceasing, the salvation of our loved ones. I confess that sometimes I do not really desire the temporal and eternal good of my relatives. Sometimes they irritate me and I don't want them to be blessed. Holy Spirit, may I always be filled with a holy love for those whom God has given to me. Jesus, let me see them and pray for them just as you see and pray for me. Pour out upon us your constant love so that we may not forget them day and night. Let every prayer be a family covenant prayer in this love of Jesus.

*In Your Name. Amen.*

Holy Spirit, we don't know how to pray as we ought. Give

72

us the right prayers to pray. Place us right in the center of the Father's will at the beginning of every prayer. Make us aware of the deep hurts and needs in those around us. Heavenly Father, we pray for true discernment, for the spiritual gifts of wisdom and knowledge so that we may know what to pray for our loved ones. Holy Spirit, reveal to us the secret tears and hidden cries of our family members. Father, you have placed the solitary in families so that each person would have someone who knows and cares about every intimate need. Forgive us our blindness and the selfishness that hides the wounds of those we love from us. Words separate but spirits can totally share. Jesus, by your Spirit of love, help us to communicate with each other. May we always speak the truth in love to each other. In the name of Him who is the Truth, Amen.

Father, sometimes it seems that we are always fighting. Jealousy, competition, suspicion and resentment more than love and unity characterize our families. Make us willing to forgive and to share. Make us able to bear one another's burdens. You have bound us together in a sacrament of unity; rebuke the flesh with which we make one another miserable. Family life could be so beautiful if we would only let the love of Christ rule in our homes. Holy Spirit, anoint our hearts and prayers so that we will see each other as gifts from God and not as rivals. Make all of us in this family true intercessors for each other. Jesus, we want to love so badly, we are so tired of hurting and being hurt, let your Agape love fill our homes. Baptize us with self-giving love. Oh, love, you are a person. Come unto our homes and sup with us.

In Your Name. Amen.

Heavenly Father, in your Word you often remind us how faithful you are to your covenant and to yourself. We be-

*lieve that you want us to be a part of that faithfulness. Bind us together in a covenant of faithfulness to your Word. You have sworn that you want to save the members of my household. Forgive me for ever doubting it. Forgive me for failing to claim your covenant faithfulness for the members of my family. When my spouse and my children begin to stray from your Word, I become angry and accuse you. Holy Spirit, show me how you are at work in the lives of my loved ones. Show me that the Father's promise must be fulfilled no matter what seems to be happening now. Jesus, I thank and praise you in advance for everything you are going to do for my loved ones. Give me the faith to see tham saved and healed right now. Through the eyes of faith let me see them praising God together and rejoicing in His love.*

*In Your Name. Amen.*

*Father, beat in my heart, flow in my blood, breathe in my lungs. Let every thought, word and deed be offered up to you. Holy Spirit, drench me, bathe me in the presence of God. Let every atom of my body praise the Lord and rejoice in His presence. Make my body to be your temple. Turn me into a living and burning prayer. Let me give myself and you no rest day and night as long as a single member of my family is not fully saved. Anoint me with a sense of urgency. Now is the appointed time. Now is the day of salvation. Now is the time to pray for my family. Let my eyes know no sleep and my spirit no rest until all your covenant promises for my family are fulfilled. Father, you have sworn it by your mighty arm and you cannot lie.*

*In Jesus' Name. Amen.*

*Father, it is difficult for us to understand that we are not individuals but actually members of each other. Let the family unity be so real to us that we can feel and understand it. Jesus, be real to us. Be so real that we can reach out and touch your face. Show us how to touch you by loving each other. Holy Spirit, show us that no man lives or dies unto himself. Let us become more aware of the links between us. Jesus, as you become real to us, become real also to the members of our bodies, our families. As we come to know and love you better, let that joy flow through the whole household. As we grow in grace, in spirit and truth, let that experience be directly shared by all those who share our blood.*

*In Your Name. Amen.*

*Holy Spirit, create in my loved ones a hunger and thirst for the Lord and His Word. I'm tired of pushing; the hard sell isn't working. Make them want to come to the Lord on their own. Jesus, you must show them how real and loving you are; I can't. All I do is turn them off to religion. Holy Spirit, I ask you not to destroy their freedom but to sneak up on them when they aren't looking and plant the seed of God in their hearts. Counteract the influence of the world on my children. Let the Father have equal time. Somehow the devil seems so much more effective in his propaganda because he speaks to the hidden traitor in our hearts. Jesus, Good Shepherd, let them hear and follow the voice of the shepherd. Block out the voice of the stranger in their lives. Show my loved ones, Jesus, that all you want is to give them more abundant life.*

*In Your Name. Amen.*

*Heavenly Father, you know what it means to lose a Son. No angel stayed the hand of death when your divine Son, Jesus, was sacrificed on the altar of the cross. Let our prayers for our loved ones rise up before you day and night. May our love for those entrusted to us be a constant burning prayer. Holy Spirit, when we forget to pray, pray within* us with signs and groans too deep for words. If we forget to pray for our loved ones, even for a moment, do not you forget. Jesus our brother, bind these our brothers and sisters, sons and daughters, parents and grandparents to us by cords of eternal love. Make constant intercession for all of us before the throne of the Father. Let Father, Son and Holy Spirit pray for my family day and night. Plug us into the cosmic prayer chain with angels and archangels and all the company of heaven.

*In Jesus' Name. Amen.*

Holy Spirit, teach us how to pray according to the will of God. Give me the right prayers to pray for this family. Show me how to love and how to understand them. Keep me from bitterness and self-pity when they seem to rebel. Give me patience to wait upon the Lord when things don't work out according to my desires. Heavenly Father, you are the judge and you command us not to judge. Show me how to be merciful and gracious just as you are. Jesus, show me how to see the highest and best in all men and particularily in the members of my family.

*In Your Name. Amen.*

Heavenly Father, you give and you take away. Teach us not to question your judgment when one of our loved ones is taken from us. May we claim the family covenant for our departed ones, believing that somehow they must all be saved because you have promised it. Let nothing separate any of us from the love of Christ. When sickness or disaster strikes, let that eternal covenant hold us together in prayer and faith. Holy Spirit, show us the great power in this family covenant and let nothing discourage us from praying it without ceasing.

*In Jesus' Name. Amen.*

## Chapter 13

# THE LORD'S PRAYER

*Lord, teach us how to pray as you taught your disciples.
Teach us how to go out from ourselves and be true intercessors. Let every prayer begin with a prayer for the prayer.
Send your Holy Spirit to make us sensitive to the needs and
pain of others. Jesus, let your own compassion fill us so that
we can mourn with you over the pain and sin of the world.
As you are present to all the world's need, be present to us
in a real and personal way. You are riddled with all human
agony; the sufferings of the world converge in you. Let them
also become personal to us through your presence. Jesus,
may your own prayers be our guide. Pray it with us now. We
thank you that you have made prayer possible by saying
with and for us, "Our Father."*

*In Your Name. Amen.*

The inevitable question is always asked, "How do I become an intercessor? How do I pray, what do I say?" In
Matthew 5:6-15 Jesus himself gives us the answer.

Intercession is not something to show off. "Go into your
room and shut the door." The intercessor is not trying to
impress anyone, including God. There is a secret wrestling
with God in the night like that of Jacob and Jesus. In the si-
lence of the night he reaches out and touches the very face
of God. Like Elijah, he is allowed to become a co-creator
with the Most High who hears in secret and reveals His answer before the world.

"Do not heap up empty phrases like the heathen do."

Do not tell God what He already knows. He knows what you need even better than you do. He knows what you really want. Jesus often prayed all night, but His prayers were almost all intercession. The one time He asked something for himself in Gethsemane, God said no. This is also true of Paul when he prayed about his thorn in the flesh. The secret reward of the intercessor is being mightily used as a channel for the will of God.

"Lord, teach us how to pray." Prayer is a holy art to be learned and a precious gift given to those who obey its laws. The Lord's Prayer is a short prayer; it has only fifty-four words in English and even less in Greek. The Aramaic original that Jesus spoke may have been even shorter. Yet it is the prayer that spans the world. It covers every human need and contingency. It is prayed over the infants in Holy Baptism, is joyously shared at a wedding and spoken as a reverent requiem at a funeral. From the cradle to the grave every human occasion, great or small, is encircled by its petitions.

In the Lord's Prayer, the "I" of petition becomes a "we" of intercession. It begins with the family circle and includes the world. There is not a single petition that focuses on self. In ever-widening circles it embraces all of mankind. We are not asking God to make us holy or to give us gifts but to use us as channels for His gracious will. The doxology, "for thine is the power and the glory for ever and ever," ties everything together for this purpose.

The secret power of the Lord's Prayer is its focus on God. This is the miracle of miracles: God asks us to pray for Him! The power of heaven and earth can be shaken when a man looks at God. When Martin Luther looked at God and said, "Here I stand," the church of Rome trembled. When Wesley looked at God, the world became his parish. When Moody, Edward and Whitefield looked at God, millions were converted.

*"Our Father who art in heaven."* We dare to look at God in prayer because God was in Christ. Jesus introduces us to the Father and the dread name of the nameless becomes "Abba"—papa. The Jews were afraid to even whisper the divine name, but in our immense leap of love Jesus teaches us to say, "Our Daddy in heaven." The ruler of the galaxies suddenly becomes closer than our own thoughts. The vast infinity of God is only a prayer's length away.

In the Lord's Prayer God is focused upon and made real. In Him all the needs of the world are opened up to us. In Jesus the groans and cries of the whole creation converge. He is riddled with the sufferings of the world. Every bullet strikes Him, every knife cuts Him, every cry, every sigh, every pain and death are His, too. He is constantly present to every great and tiny human need—even to those needs beneath our concern like the sparrow's fall. Because He is God, nothing can escape His presence, His knowledge, or His sharing. Because He is also man, He is our brother. He is Son of God and Brother Man, and in His presence we, too, can be present to all the world's need. The hand that we touch grasps every needy human hand. In Him we can grasp the hand of all mankind.

If this one prayer spans the world, how much more does it not embrace our own households! Yet it is so easy to pray for distant unknown heathen and overlook the heathen in our own households. Too often when believers are anointed by the Spirit, they want to rush out and minister to the whole world. In the meantime, the ministry in their own houses is sadly neglected. There are many great spiritual leaders who minister to millions and bypass their own households. The real test of our calling is among those who know us best. Our loved ones should be the first, not the last, to be prayed into the kingdom.

*"Hallowed be thy name."* Lord, we pray that your name

may always be made holy in this family. Let every part of this household join in the praises of angels and archangels and the whole company of heaven. Remind us constantly that we are the basic unit of the church. Join us together with the whole church on earth and in heaven. Let nothing we say or do to each other cause your holy name to be defamed. Let your name be hallowed when we work, when we play and when we worship. In the midst of the world, as each of us goes about our daily tasks, remind us that we as a family bear your holy name together. Hallowed be your name in our congregation and in the whole church. Let the bishops and presidents know that they must give an account to you. Hallowed be your name in the state and the national capitols. Let the governor, the president and the legislators and officials always be aware that they are your ministers. Hallowed be your name in all the nations of the world and cause every knee to bow at the holy name of Jesus. Amen.

*"Thy kingdom come."* Father, pour out your spirit in rich and full measure on my whole family. Let your kingdom come with power and grace to this household. Jesus, let your Spirit of love and peace fill our hearts and minds. Father, let your kingdom and not man's prevail in the church and the world. As our society becomes increasingly secularized, break through with your Spirit and destroy the kingdoms of man and Satan. Let your kingdom come to the church. Hinder and confound those who would build their own kingdoms in your name. Send your Holy Spirit to kings and to all who are in authority in order that we may lead quiet and peaceable lives in all godliness and honesty. Let your kingdom break through to all who are searching for the truth in order that all men might be saved and come to the knowledge of the truth. Come quickly, Lord Jesus, and es-

tablish your heavenly kingdom so that all suffering, injustice and rebelling might end.

In Your Name. Amen.

*"Thy will be done on earth as it is in heaven."* Father, let your will be done as perfectly among us as it is done by the angels in heaven. Let your will be done as joyfully in this family as it is done in the family of heaven. Let your will and not ours be done. Let this be a Christian marriage not based on the will and desire of man but on the will of God. Our own wills cause nothing but strife and pain. Let your holy will of love rule our hearts. Let your will and not the will of man be done in church and state. Let your will to save and to heal release all those who are in bondage to Satan and to sin. Lord Jesus, as you are now present to all the pain and hurt of the world, let those needs also be present to my prayer. Holy Spirit, as you pray within us, overcome all doubt, indifference and unbelief; let the will of God to save all men break through on the wings of this prayer.

In the Power and Love of Jesus. Amen.

*"Give us this day our daily bread."* Father, you are a generous giver. We believe that poverty, want and hunger come from the enemy. Jesus, you fed the multitudes and gave great and miraculous catches of fish, but Satan caused you to hunger in the wilderness. Give us neither poverty nor wealth, Father, but supply all our needs one day at a time. Teach us to look to the giver and not the gift and to thank you for every gift, no matter how small. Father, we know that two-thirds of the world goes to bed hungry every night. Forgive us for not caring and not sharing enough. Forgive us for taking the blessings of America for granted. Break the power of the enemy that keeps all your generous gifts from being shared throughout the world. Show us how to find a

sufficient source of cheap energy in the sea or the earth. Give us good weather and good crops that we may share our bread with the hungry. Help us to find new ways of getting food from the sea so that more of your children may not cry because of hunger.

In Jesus' Name. Amen.

*"Forgive us our trespasses as we forgive those who trespass against us."* Father, we live by your forgiveness. Teach us to live together by the same forgiveness. As we pray, forgive us our trespasses. May we all confess the sins of those who never confess their own. Teach us to mourn for the sins of the world as well as for our own. Holy Spirit, let the power of forgiveness renew this family every day. Do not let the sun go down on our wrath but let each day be a new day. Blot out the anger, the bitterness and the hurts of the past. Let us not remember the sins nor the rejections of our youth. Teach us to forgive ourselves and each other as you forgive us. Lord Jesus, may the members of this family accept themselves and each other just as you accept us. Let each one of us see himself and each other as you see us— through the eyes of forgiving love. Let us live by the gospel and accept the fact that we are accepted.

In Your Name. Amen.

*"Lead us not into temptation."* Heavenly Father, let nothing be a temptation for us. Do not let the stresses and frustrations of daily family living tempt us to anger. Let us walk in the Spirit and not in the flesh as we let down our guard in the family circle. Father, we pray for the members of our household who are tempted by the devil, the world and the flesh. Guard our youth and keep them from being misled by their peer groups. Holy Spirit, keep the word in their hearts when we must let them go. Let the precious

seed that has been planted not be snatched away by the enemy. Lord Jesus, continue the good work you have begun in the members of my family. Let none of them be lost.

In Your Name. Amen.

*"Deliver us from evil."* Father, deliver us from the evil one. Send mighty Michael with his angelic guards to keep constant watch over this household. Put the whole armor of God around this family. We pray against the evil force and all his works and all his ways. Confound and bind the enemy and let none of us be misled or deceived. We pray against ancestral bondage and the bondage of the generations. Let the guilt and the conflict of our forefathers not be used by Satan. Break the family solidarity of guilt through the blood of the cross. Protect our children from involvement with the occult or with drugs. Cover us day and night with the precious blood of Jesus.

In His Name. Amen.

*"For thine is the kingdom and the power and the glory for ever and ever, Amen."* Father, keep our vision focused on you and your glorious plan for us. May we constantly celebrate your presence in the midst of our family. We praise and thank you in advance that you have made an eternal covenant with this family. Holy Spirit, we thank you that you have called, enlightened and sanctified this household. May we never lose sight of this eternal call or give up hope for the salvation of every family member. Help us always to see God and to live in the light of eternity.

In Jesus' Name. Amen.

## CONCLUSION

The human family is God's guarantee that everyone, no

matter how lonely or unlovable, will be loved by someone. But far more important, the family covenant is a promise that everyone can have an intercessor. To be prayed for is far more important than merely to be loved and cared about.

The family covenant is also a guarantee that no matter how hopeless a family situation may appear, there is always something we can do about it. When we pray this prayer, "Save my household," we can be sure that God hears and answers because it's His own idea. The God who wants all men to be saved has given us an opportunity and a command to be an intimate part of that divine will.

The family covenant is eschatological. This means that its promise is faithful and eternal. At the final judgment when all things are weighed in the balance, God's covenant with the family will be ultimately decisive. Even though we may see little immediate change in our loved ones, because of this prayer we know that God cannot break His word: "And as for me, this is my covenant with them, says the Lord: my Spirit which is upon you, and my words which I have put in your mouth, shall not depart out of your mouth or out of the mouth of your children, or out of the mouth of your children's children, says the Lord, from this time forth and for evermore" (Isa. 59:21).

## Chapter 14

# SUBMISSION AND FAMILY PRIESTHOOD

There is no doubt that the New Testament teaches submission of wives to their husbands (see Eph. 5:22; Col. 3:18). It is also true that few biblical teachings have been abused as much as this one. In 1 Timothy 2, the position of men and women in the church is based on the order of creation and fall and not on some temporary social usages. The relationship rests squarely on Genesis 3:16: "Your desire shall be for your husband, and he shall rule over you." This is a part of the curses spoken by God after the Fall. The curse upon man, the ground, and the serpent still remains: "In the sweat of your face you shall eat bread till you return to the ground" (Gen. 3:17-19).

But how is this relationship (or curse) to be applied under the new covenant of Spirit? Certainly not as an unconditional legalistic principle.

"Pastor Prange, my husband will not let me go to church. Must I submit? My pastor says that I've got to submit to him no matter what he tells me." This is a complaint that I've heard hundreds of times.

Sometimes it is far worse. "Pastor, my husband insists that we join a mate-swapping group. He says that I have to obey no matter how I feel." Or, "My husband demands that I join with him in occult activities. What should I do?"

In other households no matter what comes up, the husbands demand that their wives unconditionally submit to their every whim. Authority without condition is tyranny. This is not a marriage; it's a dictatorship. But how are we to understand the meaning of submit? Does it cover every area? Is it unconditional? Is it law or gospel?

Ephesians 5:21 says, "Be subject to one another out of reverence for Christ." Here the submission is mutual. It's not a line but a circle—a circle of Agape love. This is the life-style of the new community of the Spirit: "Submit yourselves one to another." First submit yourselves to God and then to each other. There is no place in the Christian community for pulling rank (Matt. 23:2-11). Status seeking is a mark of those outside of God's covenant (Matt. 20:25-28). When husbands and wives submit to each other, it is to be out of reverence for Christ, not some legalistic authority or rank. Again and again Jesus says, "The greatest among you shall be your servant."

The authority and submission in the family is spiritual. The relationship between husband and wife is like Christ and the church (Eph. 5:32). The husband is the head of the wife as Christ is the head of the church (Eph. 5:23). What does the head of the church do? Give orders or make demands? No, He gives himself to the body (v. 25). As C. S. Lewis once said, "A truly spiritual marriage may be a crucifixion. Just as the church crucifies Christ, so husband and wife may often crucify one another." The husband is the head of the wife only insofar as he mediates the headship of Christ.

But how does the husband really mediate Christ in the family? In the Old Testament he was the priest of the family. According to Kittel (Theologisches Woerterbuch Zum Neuen Testament, Kohlhammer, Stuttgart, 1957, Dritter Band, p. 260), the head of every family could offer sacrifices as a priest. From Exodus 19:22-24 we may conclude that the family priesthood predated the official Levitical priesthood. According to Kittel (op. cit.), the Levitical priests were actually household priests. According to sources at the time of Judges and Kings, the fathers of the families normally offered up the sacrifices.

Kittel further states (op. cit., Band V., p. 132 f.) that the primitive church was built up out of families and households. The church consisted of the house of Stephanas (1 Cor. 1:16), Philemon (Acts 11:14), Cornelius (Acts 16:15), Lydia (Acts 16:31), the jailer of Philippi (Acts 16:31-34), and Crispus (Acts 18:8). The same was true of the house of Onesiphorus in 2 Timothy 1:16 and 4:19. Acts 2:46 says that bread was broken (communion celebrated) in the homes. Acts 5:42 tells us that the good news was proclaimed in the temple and in the houses. It is also made clear in these instances that the conversion of the father brought about the conversion of the entire household. There is no question that the primitive church was a house church and that the head of the family functioned as priest of that basic congregation.

As priest of the family, the father is not a dictator, rather, he is an intercessor. Dietrich Bonhoeffer once said, "Pastors are the intercessors for their congregations and not the accusers or judges. God is the judge and Satan is the accuser, and if the pastor fails to be an intercessor the congregation has none." In the same way the father of a family is to function as its intercessor. He is not to accuse or judge his wife and children but to constantly lift them up to the Lord in prayer. That's what true headship means. Anything less than that is a travesty.

There is another passage that speaks about the relationship between men and women in the church. Galatians 3:28 says, "There is neither Jew nor Greek, there is neither slave nor free, there is neither male nor female; for you are all one in Christ Jesus." Women's Lib has become largely a battle between men and women. This competition between male and female ought not to be brought into the church.

The spiritual order transcends the natural structure when- ever there are truly spiritual men and women. When we walk in the Spirit, we are already walking in the dimension of eternal life through the *arabon*, downpayment, of Spirit, In heaven all cultural and formal distinctions will be swal- lowed up in the total unity of the Spirit.

## CONCLUSION

As a Lutheran the author comes from the tradition of in- fant baptism. I believe this to be scriptural and also in con- formity with much of the history of the early church. At the same time I am very much aware that much of reformed and evangelical Christianity is committed to a divergent baptismal tradition. Many, many times I have wondered, often out loud, just where these two positions could con- verge.

The family covenant suggests one possible answer to this agonizing problem. Without resolving the conflict it- self, it offers hope and comfort to those who hold to infant as well as believers' baptism. There are two obvious objec- tions to infant baptism: first, the child cannot really parti- cipate; and secondly, there is in many cases no follow- through. Here the intercession of the family covenant cov- ers both needs. The infant is taken up into the intercession of the parents and godparents. In addition to this the fol- low-through is a response of the Spirit to the family inter- cession.

In the case of believers' baptism, the burning question has always been: if baptism is necessary for salvation, what happens to those children who die before the age of faith? If they are members of Christian families, then this problem does not really exist. According to 1 Corinthians 7:14, they are covered by the sanctification of one or both believing parents. This occurs whether they are formally dedicated or not. In 1 Corinthians 7:14, neither baptism nor dedication are mentioned as the source of the children's holiness. The mere fact that they are members of a family when one parent is a believer is enough. This is fully consistent with the thesis of the book, "Believe on the Lord Jesus Christ and you will be saved and your household."

My second concern in the book is that the impression not be left that family members can be saved against their will through the family covenant prayer. My wife is always concerned that people might be robbed of their freedom by this prayer. Actually we do not have a freedom to believe without God's prior invitation. But we always have a freedom not to believe. God knows "unfaith" as well as faith. As long as I did not believe that God healed today, He healed no one through my prayers. Jesus stands at the door and knocks. By ourselves we cannot say, "Come in," but we can always say, "Keep out." The family covenant prayer in no way removes that power of the flesh to say a final no to God. Nothing can possibly separate us from the love of God in Christ Jesus except we ourselves.

# BIBLIOGRAPHY

Barclay, William. *New Testament Words*. Philadelphia: The Westminster Press, 1964.

Bennett, Dennis & Rita. *The Holy Spirit & You*. Plainfield, New Jersey: Logos, International, 1972.

Bonhoeffer, Dietrich. *Life Together*. New York: Harper & Brothers' Publishers, 1954.

Christenson, Larry. *The Christian Family*. Minneapolis, Minnesota: Bethany Fellowship, Inc.,1970.

Donne, John. *Devotions*. The University of Michigan Press: Ann Arbor paperback, 1959.

Ebersheim, Alfred. *The Life and Times of Jesus the Messiah*. Grand Rapids, Michigan: Wm. B. Eerdmans Publishing Company, 1953.

Ellis, Albert, and Harper, Robert A. *A Guide to Successful Marriage*. California: Wilshire Book Company, 1961.

Ford, Marvin. *On the Other Side*. Plainfield, New Jersey: Logos, International, 1978.

Garvin Lectures. *In Search of God*. Boston: Beacon Press, 1961.

Grubb, Norman. *Rees Howells, Intercessor*. Ft. Washington, Pennsylvania: Christian Literature Crusade, 1973.

Hong, Edna. *Bright Valley of Love*. Minneapolis, Minnesota: Augsburg Publishing House, 1976.

Jeremias, Joachim. *Infant Baptism in the First Four Centuries*. London: SCM Press, LTD, 1964.

Jeremias, Joachim. *The Origins of Infant Baptism*. London: SCM Press, LTD, 1963.

Kallas, James, *The Real Satan*. Minneapolis, Minnesota: Augsburg Publishing House, 1975.

Lejeune, R. *Christoph Blumhardt and His Message.* Woodcrest, Rifton, New York: The Plough Publishing House, 1963.

Lewis, C. S. *A Mind Awake.* New York: Harcourt, Brace & World, Inc., 1969.

MacNutt, Francis. *The Power to Heal.* Notre Dame, Indiana: Ave Maria Press, 1977.

Martin, Del. *Battered Wives.* New York: Pocket Books, 1977.

Matson, Archie. *Afterlife.* New York: Harper & Row, Publishers, 1977.

Malz, Betty. *My Glimpse of Eternity.* Waco, Texas: Chosen Books, Inc., 1978.

Montgomery, John Warwick. *Demon Possession.* Minneapolis, Minnesota: Bethany Fellowship, Inc., 1976.

Moody, D. L. *Heaven.* Chicago: The Moody Press.

Moody, Jr., Raymond A. *Life After Life.* New York: Bantam, 1977.

Mow, Anna B. *Your Child From Birth to Rebirth.* Grand Rapids, Michigan: Zondervan Publishing House, 1974.

Mudd, Emily Hartshorne and Krich, Aron. *Man and Wife.* New York: W. W. Norton & Company, Inc., 1957.

Nelson, Elof. *Prime Time.* Owatonna, Minnesota: Journal-Chronicle Co., 1971.

Osis, Karlis and Haraldsson, Erlendur. *At the Hour of Death.* New York: Avon Books, 1977.

Patterson, Gerald R. *Families.* Champaign, Illinois: Research Press, 1975.

Saarnivaara, Uuras. *Scriptural Baptism.* New York: Vantage Press, Inc., 1953.

Sandberg, Anne. *Seeing the Invisible.* Plainfield, New Jersey: Logos International, 1977.

Sanford, Agnes. *Creation Waits.* Plainfield, New Jersey: Logos International, 1978.

Scanlan, Michael. *The Power in Penance.* Notre Dame, Indiana: Ave Maria Press, 1972.

Schaeffer, Francis A. *How Should We Then Live?* Old Tappan, New Jersey: Fleming H. Revell Company, 1976.

Schaeffer, Francis A. *True Spirituality.* Wheaton, Illinois: Tyndale House Publishers, 1973.

Snaith, Norman H. *The Distinctive Ideas of the Old Testament.* London: The Epworth Press, 1953.

Stewart, Charles William. *The Minister As Marriage Counselor.* New York: Abingdon Press, 1961.

Wheeler, David R. *Life After Death.* New York: Grosset & Dunlap Company, 1977.

White, John Wesley. *Re-Entry.* Grand Rapids, Michigan: Zondervan Publishing House, 1972.